FAITH-BASED
INSIDE THE MINDS OF SEX TRAFFICKING VICTIMS

Faith-Based Inside the Minds of Sex Trafficking Victims

This book is set in the typeface *Work Sans* designed by Wei Huang.

Paperback ISBN: 979-8-39026-00-36

A Publication of *Tall Pine Books*
119 E Center Street, Suite B4A | Warsaw, Indiana 46580
www.tallpinebooks.com

| 2 25 23 20 16 02 |

Published in the United States of America

FAITH-BASED INSIDE THE MINDS OF SEX TRAFFICKING VICTIMS

Training Manual for Christian Counselors, Safe Homes, Nonprofits, Churches, and Faith-Based Service Providers

SULA LAEL

CONTENTS

INTRODUCTION

Welcome Friend,

I'm deeply honored that you've picked up this book. Whether you're a Christian counselor, safe home leader, nonprofit director, ministry worker, intercessor, or someone simply moved by compassion—thank you. Your willingness to grow in understanding the realities of sex trafficking and to walk with survivors in their healing journey is both rare and urgently needed.

This book was born from two deeply intertwined sources: my own lived experience as a survivor of sex trafficking and ritual abuse, and over a decade of working across the continuum of care in the anti-trafficking movement. In 2022, I founded *Take Flight Survivors*, a 501(c)(3) nonprofit committed to embracing survivors with support, encouragement, and spiritual care as they transition from slavery into safety, freedom, and restoration.

I didn't write this book to simply inform you—I wrote it to *equip you.* My prayer is that it helps you minister from a place that is Holy Spirit-led, trauma-informed, survivor-informed, and rooted in deep compassion.

While many anti-trafficking resources stop at awareness or surface-level training, *Faith-Based: Inside the Minds of Sex Trafficking Survivors* goes further. Through a Kingdom lens, I gently guide you into some of the deeper, often hidden dynamics that survivors live with daily—things like complex trauma, dissociation, mind control programming, spiritual bondage, Satanic Ritual Abuse (SRA), and occult crimes. These are difficult realities, but they are not rare. I've lived them, and I've walked closely with others who have too. This book gives language to what many survivors have not yet been able to speak.

If you're ready to go even deeper, this book also serves as a companion to the online course *Ministering to Sex Trafficking Survivors*, available through Take Flight Academy. The course expands on these topics with practical tools and ministry strategies to help you walk in both wisdom and Kingdom authority— whether your role is in housing, counseling, advocacy, deliverance, or pastoral care.

You can access the course here:
www.TakeFlightSurvivors.org/Academy

At *Take Flight Survivors*, we believe that the journey from bondage to breakthrough must be wrapped in love, wisdom, and the power of the Holy Spirit. We train service providers in trauma-informed care that honors the voice of survivors, while equipping them with biblically grounded, Spirit-empowered tools for healing. No two healing journeys are the same—and there are no one-size-fits-all answers. Only Jesus.

Throughout Scripture, Jesus ministered in uniquely personal ways. He said and did only what He saw the Father doing (John 5:19; John 12:49). We must do the same—ministering with sensitivity, listening to both the Holy Spirit and the survivor, and creating space for freedom through choice, not control.

It's crucial to remember this: forcing faith on someone who isn't ready can cause harm. Survivors need to encounter the *real* Jesus—not religion, pressure, or performance. That encounter must be wrapped in love, patience, kindness, and humility.

My heart's cry is that every survivor would come to know the finished work of the Cross, discover how deeply they are loved, and rise in their identity as sons and daughters of the King.

By the time you finish this book, I pray you'll be better equipped to recognize trafficking situations, respond wisely, and minister with compassion and Holy Spirit power. You are stepping into sacred work—and I'm truly grateful you've answered the call.

With honor and gratitude,

Sula Lael
Founder, Take Flight Survivors
www.TakeFlightSurvivors.org
www.SulaLael.com

PART ONE: SEX TRAFFICKING

CHAPTER 1

WHAT IS SEX TRAFFICKING?

Sex trafficking is a form of modern-day slavery where individuals are forced, coerced, or deceived into the commercial sex trade against their will. It includes any child involved in commercial sex. Sex traffickers often target vulnerable individuals with a history of abuse and use violence, threats, lies, false promises, debt bondage, or other forms of control and manipulation to keep victims involved in the sex industry.

Service providers need to understand the types of sex trafficking in America and be aware of the facts and statistics surrounding this issue. This knowledge will help them identify victims and provide appropriate support.

TYPES OF SEX TRAFFICKING IN AMERICA

There are many forms of sex trafficking. Below are some of the most commonly identified:

1. Intimate partner trafficking, where the trafficker is a romantic partner or spouse.
2. Familial trafficking, where the trafficker is a family member.
3. Illicit massage business (brothel) trafficking, where the trafficker operates a front business, such as a massage parlor, to hide the sex trafficking that takes place.
4. Child sexual abuse material (CSAM) trafficking, where children are exploited to produce explicit content that is recorded, distributed, or sold for profit. This abuse may occur in organized rings or by individuals who sell material online.
5. Pornography trafficking, where individuals are forced or coerced to perform in pornography against their will.
6. Occult crime/satanic ritual abuse (SRA) trafficking, where victims are subjected to ritual abuse in combination with sexual exploitation.
7. Strip club/topless bar/cantina trafficking, where individuals are forced to work in these establishments and are exploited through commercial sex acts.
8. Online exploitation and cybersex trafficking, where traffickers use livestreams, webcams, or digital communication to exploit victims, often involving threats, coercion, or the sale of

explicit content involving children or vulnerable individuals.

9. Survival sex trafficking, where individuals, often youth or those experiencing homelessness, are coerced or manipulated into sex acts in exchange for basic needs like food, shelter, protection, or transportation.

10. Gang-controlled trafficking, where a victim is trafficked by a gang as part of its criminal enterprise, often involving extreme violence, control, and community intimidation.

11. Escort service trafficking, where traffickers pose as legitimate escort agencies but force individuals into commercial sex under the guise of legal work.

FACTS AND STATISTICS

It is challenging to find accurate statistics and facts about sex trafficking, as it is underreported. However, it is important to understand the scope of the issue. Some statistics and facts include:

- The United States is one of the top 3 nations in which trafficking originates. -U.S. Dept. of State Trafficking In Persons Report
- Top 3 States in the USA where Sex Trafficking is Reported 1. California 2. Texas 3. Florida -Polaris
- Studies consistently report that 50-90% of child sex trafficking victims have been involved in the child welfare system. -Child Welfare Information Gateway

- The United States is a source, transit, and destination country for men, women, transgender individuals, and children—both U.S. citizens and foreign nationals— subjected to sex trafficking and forced labor. -U.S. Dept. of State T.I.P.
- Every 2 minutes, a child is being prepared for sexual exploitation. -UNICEF
- There are girls as young as 5 and 6 years old in the U.S. who are forced to do sexual acts for economic gain by their pimp. –U.S. Department of Justice
- In some cases, children may be born into sex trafficking, or be forced into it as a toddler. Sex trafficking of those who are younger than 10 years old when they entered that life is perpetrated almost exclusively by family members, often a father or stepfather. -THORN.org
- The average age a girl enters the commercial sex trade is 12-14 years old. For boys, it's even younger, just 11-13 years old. -National Center for Missing and Exploited Children
- 4,500,000 are being trafficked for forced labor through sexual exploitation every year; this is in addition to the millions already held captive by trafficking. –ILO
- Each year, as many as 100,000-300,000 American children are at risk of being trafficked for commercial sex in the United States. -U.S. Department of Justice
- Field research in nine countries concluded that 60-75% of women in prostitution were raped,

70-95% were physically assaulted, and 68% met the criteria for Post Traumatic Stress Disorder in the same range as treatment-seeking combat veterans. -Farley, Melissa et al. 2003. "Prostitution and Trafficking in Nine Countries: An Update on Violence and Posttraumatic Stress Disorder." Journal of Trauma Practice

- 70% of female trafficking victims are trafficked into the commercial sex industry, including porn, stripping, and legal brothels. -US Department of Justice, Assessment of US Government Activities to Combat Trafficking in Persons

- Up to 95% have a history of childhood sexual abuse. -Melissa Farley, Prostitution and Sexual Violence Psychiatric Times

- A study published in the scientific Journal of Trauma Practice found that 89% of women in prostitution wanted to escape but had no other means of survival.

- A 2025 report from the Department of Health and Human Services revealed that over 291,000 unaccompanied minors were released into the U.S without proper tracking, leaving them vulnerable to exploitation by gangs and cartels. 32,000 failed to appear in court after release. Whistleblowers have highlighted inadequate vetting processes, with some sponsors turning out to be traffickers or criminals.

- According to Polaris, 1 in 7 of the children reported to the National Center for Missing and Exploited Children became victims of sexual trafficking. Of this number, 88 percent were coming out of the foster care system.

GLOSSARY OF TRAFFICKING AND PIMP CULTURE TERMS

Glossary of Trafficking & Pimp Culture Terms
1. 403 / Four-Oh-Three
    A code word used to refer to a "hoe" or prostituted person. Some pimps use numerical slang to mask conversations from outsiders.

2. Bottom (or Bottom B*)
    The trafficker's most trusted girl, usually a victim who helps manage or recruit other girls, enforces rules, and collects money. She is still being exploited, but may be perceived to have "status."

3. Stable
    The group of prostituted individuals or trafficking victims under the control of a single pimp or trafficker.

4. Quota
    The amount of money a victim is expected to earn in a day or night. If they don't meet it, consequences like violence, withholding food, or emotional manipulation and abuse may follow.

5. Turn Out
   The process of initiating someone into prostitution or trafficking. A pimp may refer to "turning someone out" as a way of breaking them in.

6. Choose Up
   A victim is said to "choose up" when she leaves one pimp for another, often under pressure or manipulation. This is falsely presented as a "choice" but is often coerced or forced.

7. Reckless Eyeballing
   A street term used when someone makes eye contact with another pimp's girl or a victim makes eye contact with another pimp. This is seen as disrespectful and could result in violence.

8. Gorilla Pimp
   A trafficker who uses physical violence and intimidation to control victims. Known for brutality, as opposed to a "Romeo pimp" who uses charm and false love.

9. Romeo Pimp / Loverboy
   A trafficker who uses emotional manipulation, romance, or false promises of love to lure and control victims. This involves love bombing, gaslighting, coercion, and manipulation.

10. Wifey / Wife-in-Law
    Other girls, working for the same pimp. Victims may refer to one another this way, especially if they are trafficked as part of a stable.

11. Out of Pocket
    A victim is said to be "out of pocket" when she is disobeying her pimp, working independently, or talking to another trafficker.

12. Circuit
    A series of cities or locations where trafficked individuals are taken to be sold. Common circuits exist across the U.S. and are rotated to avoid detection.

13. Family / Folks
    Slang used within pimp culture to refer to the trafficker and their victims, often in a distorted "family" dynamic that reinforces loyalty and control.

14. Choosing Fee / Choose Fee
    Money a new pimp pays to take control of a victim from another pimp, or what a girl must pay to leave a pimp (often dangerous or impossible due to debt bondage).

15. Breaking / Seasoning
    The intentional use of trauma, rape, violence, or degradation to "break" a victim's will and make them more compliant.

16. Track / Blade / Stroll
    Street terms for areas where prostitution and trafficking activity is concentrated. For example: "She's out on the blade tonight."

17. Daddy / Poppa
    A term many victims are forced to use to refer to their pimp or trafficker, creating psychological dependence and distorted attachment.

18. Square / Green
    Someone who is not part of "the life" (i.e., trafficking or street culture). Often used to describe people who don't understand pimp culture.

19. Game / The Life
    The culture, rules, and lifestyle of prostitution and trafficking. Survivors often refer to being "in the life" or "leaving the game."

20. Trap House / Spot
    A place where victims are kept, often against their will, and where buyers come for sexual exploitation. This location is a place where drugs are sold as well.

HOW DO TRAFFICKERS FIND NEW VICTIMS?

Traffickers often use online platforms to research and target their victims. They may set up fake profiles on social media, dating sites, and gaming systems to gain the trust of their victims. In-person, traffickers look for vulnerabilities and traumas to exploit. They seek to fill a need in the grooming process so that they can make their new victim believe that they are indebted to them and demand sexual acts for repayment. Traffickers also look for individuals who are easy to manipulate and control, such as run-aways, foster children, people struggling with sub-stance abuse, international immigrant workers, and students.

RED FLAGS TO SHARE WITH OTHERS

1. Dreams being sold to you that seem too good to be true: Traffickers often offer their victims the promise of a better life, such as a job op-portunity or a chance to travel to a new city or country. These offers can be very attractive and lure unsuspecting individuals into a dangerous situation.

2. New "friends" online: Traffickers use social media and other online platforms to find and target potential victims. They may use fake pro-files to befriend individuals and gain their trust. Service providers need to be aware of this and promote online safety by encouraging people to be cautious when accepting friend requests and to limit personal information that is shared online.

3. A free, one-way ticket being given to you for a fun trip or a business opportunity: Traffickers often lure their victims by offering them a free

trip or a job opportunity, but once they arrive at the destination, they are forced into trafficking.

4. Someone much older, whom you don't really know, taking an interest in dating you and spoiling you with lots of free stuff: Traffickers often manipulate their victims by pretending to be in a romantic relationship with them. They shower them with gifts and compliments to create a sense of dependence and attachment.

5. When someone tries to isolate you from family and friends to convince you to be in a relationship solely dependent on them: Traffickers often use isolation as a tactic to control their victims. They may convince them to cut off contact with their family and friends, making them more vulnerable to exploitation.

6. Anytime you get into drugs: Traffickers often use drugs to control their victims, making them more compliant and easier to manipulate. The drug trade is also often connected to sex trafficking.

7. Underage drinking at parties: Young people are often targeted by traffickers at parties where they may be drugged, raped, and exploited.

8. A new job that pressures you to quickly relocate: Traffickers often offer jobs that require their victims to move to a new city or country, making it harder for them to escape.

9. Abusive relationships can also potentially lead to sexual exploitation: Abusive partners may use coercion or violence to force their victims

into sex acts with others, for their financial gain. This is trafficking.

10. Being in a relationship with someone addicted to pornography is a risk: Pornography addiction can lead to a desire to act out fantasies in real life, and victims may be forced into sexual acts they are uncomfortable with.

11. Being lured to catch a ride with a stranger: Traffickers may offer their victims a ride, and once they are in the car, they are forced into slavery.

12. Running away from home puts you at risk: Runaway youth are often targeted by traffickers who offer them a place to stay, food, and money, only to exploit them later.

HOW TO EDUCATE MINORS ABOUT TRAFFICKING

One of the most common questions I hear from parents and caregivers is, "How do I talk to my child about trafficking?" As a survivor and someone who's worked closely with exploited minors, I've seen firsthand how vital it is to create a home environment free from shame and judgment. When kids and teens know that they can come to you without fear of punishment or overreaction, they're more likely to share when something feels off or unsafe.

Imagine your child encountering something disturbing online or in person. If they know they can tell you about a creepy message or a scary encounter without getting in trouble, they'll come to you. For example, if they come to you to get help because a nasty man sent them a picture of their genitalia through social media, would you take their phone and punish them? Or would you help navigate the situation, providing steps of safety without punishing them for their vulnerability and openness with you? That open line of communication can make all the difference in protecting them from predators.

When you talk about trafficking, do it in a way that empowers rather than terrifies. Help them understand that there are people out there who might pretend to be kind but have bad intentions—people who want to use others' bodies for their own financial gain. By educating them about red flags and encouraging them to trust their instincts, you equip them with the tools to stay safe.

Also, consider implementing practical safety measures, such as parental control apps and having a pre-arranged code word or emoji for emergencies. This way, your child can signal for help discreetly if they ever feel unsafe. And remember, the goal is to create a culture of trust and openness, where your child knows they can always come to you for support and prayer, without fear of judgment.

IDENTIFYING VICTIMS

Some identifiers that may indicate a person is a victim of trafficking include:

1. A reluctance to make eye contact: Trafficking victims may avoid making eye contact, which can be a sign of fear or shame.
2. Another person speaking for them: If someone else is speaking for the person, it may indicate that they're not in control of their own life.
3. Lack of control over identification: If a person doesn't have control over their identification documents or other personal information, it could be a sign of trafficking.
4. Tattoos or branding: Traffickers may brand their victims with tattoos, which can serve as a sign of ownership.
5. Scripted or rehearsed responses: Victims may be coached on what to say and how to act in order to avoid detection.
6. Signs of physical abuse: Unexplained bruises or other injuries may be a sign of physical abuse.
7. Submissive or fearful: Trafficking victims may be fearful or overly submissive, particularly around their traffickers.
8. Appearing destitute/lacking personal possessions: Victims may not have personal possessions or money of their own.
9. Working excessively long hours: Victims may work long hours with no breaks or time off.
10. Living with their employer or at their job: Trafficking victims may live with their traffickers or be forced to live on the premises where they work.

It's important to note that any child or teen involved in the sex industry is a victim of trafficking, regardless of whether or not they exhibit the above identifiers. It's crucial that service providers remain alert and vigilant in their efforts to identify and assist victims of sex trafficking.

STATEMENTS A SURVIVOR MAY MAKE WHEN THEY DON'T REALIZE THEY'VE BEEN TRAFFICKED YET

Many victims of sex trafficking do not self-identify as victims—especially in the early stages of recovery or disclosure. This is often due to deeply ingrained shame, confusion, and psychological manipulation. Some may still blame themselves for what happened, believing they were complicit or that it was "just abuse" rather than trafficking. Others may not yet recognize that the person who exploited them was a trafficker—especially when a trauma bond has been formed. These internal conflicts, combined with cultural narratives and a lack of accurate language, can make it difficult for survivors to see their experiences clearly.

- "I used to have a sugar daddy who paid my bills, but sometimes he'd loan me out to his friends when I couldn't keep up."
- "I thought we were just making content together for OnlyFans, but then he started forcing me to do things on camera I didn't agree to."

- "I was sexually abused. When I lived with my aunt and uncle, their friends would come over and 'babysit' me. They always gave my uncle cash."

- "I met a guy online who said he loved me. He flew me out, but once I got there, he took my phone and made me start working at a club."

- "My mom told me it was just something our family did to survive. She said I owed it to her to help pay the rent."

- "I thought I was working as an escort to support myself, but my manager kept all the money and said I had to work it off."

- "When I ran away, I didn't have anywhere to go. This older guy let me stay with him, but then he started bringing guys over."

- "I used to hang out at parties where the older guys would drug us and pass us around. I just thought that's what happened when you partied too hard."

- "At first, I wanted to dance to make money, but then my boyfriend said if I loved him, I'd do extras in the backroom for his cut."

- "I was convinced to be in a poly relationship. He said it was spiritual and freeing, but I was the only one he made sleep with other people for money."

- "My foster dad used to say I was his favorite. He gave me gifts, but only if I let him do things to me. He recorded it and let his friends watch."

- "We were part of a church that had secret rituals. I didn't think it was wrong until I got older and realized I was being touched by grown men during them."

- "My trafficker said it wasn't trafficking because I said yes. But I only said yes because I was scared of what would happen if I didn't."

PERSONAL PRAYER PROMPTS

1. Lord, open my eyes.
   I ask You to awaken my eyes and heart to see what I have not seen before. Help me recognize the signs of trafficking and understand the realities without fear or denial. Make me alert, compassionate, and courageous.

2. Heal my heart, Lord.
   If I have experienced trauma or exploitation in any form, I invite You into those places. I give You my pain, confusion, and shame. Please bring deep healing to every wound and restore what was taken.

3. Use me to intercede for the hurting.
   I lift up every child, teen, and adult who is still trapped in trafficking. I ask You to send help. Send Your angels. Open a way of escape. Let justice prevail and deliverance break through.

4. Help me create safety for others.
   Lord, help me be someone who creates safety, not shame. Teach me how to speak with love,

to listen without judgment, and to be a trusted person for the vulnerable around me.

5. Protect the innocent.
   I pray for every child at risk—those in the foster system, on the streets, or being groomed online. Surround them with protection. Interrupt every plan of the enemy and draw them into Your covering love.

6. Strengthen those who serve.
   I lift up the service providers, first responders, counselors, and advocates. Fill them with wisdom, endurance, and Your Spirit. Help me support them however You lead.

7. Break cultural deception.
   I renounce any lies I've believed that normalize or glamorize exploitation. Help me recognize unhealthy patterns and influences in media, relationships, and community. Let truth shape my thinking.

8. Jesus, what do you want to say to me, show me, or reveal to me? (Wait on the Lord in His presence. Journal what you see, hear, or feel He is revealing to you.)

NOTES

CHAPTER 2

UNDERSTANDING THE PSYCHOLOGY OF TRAFFICKERS

While many view traffickers as pure predators, it's important to understand that many traffickers were once victims themselves. A significant number of traffickers, especially those operating in familial or generational trafficking rings, were sexually abused as children. This unhealed trauma can fester into cycles of control, power-seeking, and exploitation of others. Rather than confronting their pain, some choose to reenact it, turning their own victimization into a strategy for dominance.

In addition to personal histories of abuse, traffickers often emerge from environments where the exploitation of women and children has been normalized. Cultural messages—particularly in music, pornography, and media—glorify pimp culture, hypersexualize children, and desensitize audiences to violence and domination. Songs that praise the power of the "pimp" and reduce women to sexual objects aren't just entertainment; they are programming. These messages reinforce the narcissistic worldview of traffickers, who often justify their actions by convincing themselves that their victims "want it," "chose this life," or "owe them."

Moreover, when society sexualizes children through fashion trends, viral content, and lenient legal frameworks, it creates fertile ground for exploitation. The trafficker's grooming becomes easier in a world already primed to see minors as mature or sexually available. For this reason, it is crucial to expose not only individual trafficking cases but also the broader cultural frameworks that support and sustain them.

Understanding these factors doesn't excuse traffickers' actions, but it equips us to disrupt the root systems and societal structures that breed exploitation. True justice and prevention come not only through legal intervention, but through cultural repentance and transformation. As we dismantle these mindsets, we also pave the way for healing—not just for victims, but potentially even for former perpetrators willing to confront their brokenness, repent and convert their lives to faith in Jesus.

We are living in a day and time when not only are our children being sexualized, but there is a growing agenda to protect those who seek to abuse and exploit them. It is a grotesque and evil distortion to frame pedophilia as a "sexual preference" worthy of protection or acceptance. This ideology is not only from the pit of hell, but it endangers children and empowers predators. No individual who tolerates or normalizes this thinking can truly claim to value justice or innocence.

TRAFFICKERS ARE NARCISSISTS

Understanding the psychology of traffickers is crucial for recognizing the dynamics at play in sex trafficking. Most traffickers exhibit strong narcissistic traits, using coercive control, psychological warfare, and manipulation to dominate their victims. These tactics mirror those identified in Biderman's Chart of Coercion, which outlines methods like isolation, monopolizing perception, induced exhaustion, threats, occasional kindness, demonstrating control, humiliation, and trivial demands. These methods, originally documented in studies of prisoners of war, highlight how traffickers systematically break down their victims' will and sense of self.

TYPES OF NARCISSISTIC TRAFFICKERS

- Covert Narcissists (The "Romeo" Trafficker): These traffickers often appear charming, loving, and supportive, winning the trust of their victims and those around them. Publicly, they may seem like the perfect partner or friend, but behind closed doors, they are emotionally and psychologically manipulative, using affection as a tool of control.

- Overt Narcissists (The "Gorilla" Trafficker): These traffickers are openly domineering and abusive. They rely on intimidation, physical violence, and threats to maintain power and control. They often display grandiose self-importance, entitlement, and lack empathy for others.

- Malignant Narcissists ("Familial" Trafficking): In cases of familial trafficking, the traffickers often exhibit malignant narcissism, which combines extreme narcissistic traits with aggression, sadism, and a complete lack of empathy. These traffickers may be parents or relatives who exploit the child for financial gain, power, or other benefits. They often operate under a veil of secrecy and manipulation, making it incredibly difficult for the victim to recognize the abuse. This type of trafficker can also exhibit covert narcissistic traits, presenting themselves as caring or victimized to outsiders while secretly abusing and exploiting the child. The betrayal of trust in a familial context makes this form of trafficking especially insidious and damaging.

KEY NARCISSISTIC ABUSE TACTICS

- Love Bombing: At the beginning of the relationship, traffickers may overwhelm their victims with flattery, affection, attention, and gifts. This grooming and intense display of false "love" creates an emotional high and a sense of loyalty. Once attachment is formed, the trafficker begins to devalue, manipulate, and exploit the victim.

- Gaslighting: This tactic involves causing the victim to doubt their memories, perceptions, or sanity. Traffickers use gaslighting to disorient their victims and make them feel dependent and confused. Gaslighting is master manipulation and conditioning/programming. The victim is always wrong and the trafficker is always right. An individual can gaslight without even realizing it, especially when they are desperate to protect their narrative and avoid accountability. In doing so, they instinctively shift blame onto the victim, justifying their abuse and reinforcing control.

- Smear Campaigns: Traffickers often spread lies or distorted narratives about their victims to others. This damages the victim's reputation, isolates them from support systems, and makes it more difficult for them to seek help or be believed.

- Flying Monkeys: Traffickers may use others to do their bidding and enforce control over the victim. These "flying monkeys" can be friends, relatives, or even strangers who believe the trafficker's version of events. They help reinforce the trafficker's narrative, further isolating and controlling the victim. In some cases, this includes the trafficker's own parents or family members, making the survivor feel outnumbered, invalidated, and trapped. Flying Monkeys often use gaslighting tactics as well to protect the pimp or trafficker.

By understanding these dynamics, survivors and those supporting them can better recognize the signs of narcissistic abuse and gain insight into the psychological control that often keeps victims bound. It's also important to recognize that prolonged exposure to such abuse can lead survivors to develop antisocial behaviors or coping mechanisms that were necessary for survival. These learned behaviors can be misunderstood if not seen through a trauma-informed lens.

For service providers and compassionate individuals working with survivors, it's essential to help them identify patterns of narcissistic abuse—not just from traffickers, but also in future relationships. Some survivors may feel tempted to tolerate a toxic relationship if it seems "not as bad" as their trafficking experience. But emotional and psychological abuse in any form is still abuse. Helping survivors understand the full spectrum of narcissistic manipulation empowers them to set boundaries, rebuild their self-worth, and avoid repeating patterns of exploitation.

Recognizing that traffickers' behavior stems from a distorted self-perception and need for control, not anything the victim did, also helps dismantle the shame survivors may carry. The abuse they endured was never their fault.

BIBLICAL EXAMPLES OF NARCISSISTS

Pharaoh – The Narcissistic Trafficker:
Pharaoh wasn't just a ruler with a hard heart—he was a trafficker. He enslaved the Hebrew people,

exploiting their labor to build his empire (Exodus 1:11-14). His treatment of them was cruel and calculated, including harsh physical labor and violent population control, such as ordering the murder of Hebrew baby boys (Exodus 1:15-22). Like many modern traffickers, Pharaoh operated from entitlement, pride, and control. When Moses, sent by God, demanded freedom for the Israelites, Pharaoh repeatedly hardened his heart (Exodus 7:13, 8:15), gaslit Moses with false promises (Exodus 8:28-29), and retaliated by increasing the people's burdens (Exodus 5:6-9). His narcissism was rooted in power and self-glorification, refusing to acknowledge God's authority even in the face of divine judgment.

King Saul – The Insecure Narcissist:

King Saul began as a humble man (1 Samuel 9:21), but his deep insecurity grew into a controlling and jealous narcissism. When David began gaining favor and popularity, Saul felt threatened and became obsessed with preserving his image and status. He tried multiple times to kill David (1 Samuel 18:10-11, 19:1, 19:9-10), despite David's loyalty and honor toward him. Saul's actions reflect a narcissistic need to eliminate perceived threats rather than address inner brokenness. He valued his reputation more than righteousness (1 Samuel 15:30) and often viewed others through the lens of rivalry, not relationship.

Jezebel – The Controlling Occult Manipulator:

Jezebel exemplifies the narcissistic abuser who thrives on manipulation, deception, and domination. She orchestrated the murder of Naboth simply because he refused to sell his vineyard to King Ahab (1 Kings 21:1-16). She used lies, forged letters, and public humiliation to destroy an innocent man—all to gain power and satisfy her selfish desires. Jezebel also relentlessly persecuted God's prophets, seeking to silence truth and elevate Baal worship (1 Kings 18:4, 19:1-2). Her tactics mirror the psychological abuse of narcissistic traffickers today: calculated schemes, character assassination, and a complete disregard for truth or justice.

The Pharisees – Religious Narcissists:

The Pharisees often displayed narcissistic traits cloaked in religious zeal. They were more concerned with appearances than substance (Matthew 23:5-7), and they exploited their religious authority to control others rather than serve them (Matthew 23:2-4). They frequently tried to trap Jesus with twisted questions (Matthew 22:15-18), plotted His death out of envy (Mark 15:10), and used their spiritual influence to shame and silence the vulnerable (John 8:3-5). Their refusal to repent or receive correction revealed a rigid self-righteousness and fear of losing control—hallmarks of narcissistic behavior. They didn't just oppose Jesus; they resented Him for threatening their dominance.

The legalistic leaders of Jesus' day were the only people He consistently confronted, corrected, and rebuked. In Matthew 23:13 (TPT), Jesus says, "Great sorrow awaits you, religious scholars and you Pharisees—frauds and pretenders! For you obstruct people's access to the kingdom of heaven's realm. You refuse to enter in, and you block the way for those who want to enter." These leaders had outward displays of holiness (covert narcissists) but lacked the heart of God, making it difficult for others to experience the freedom, love, and power of the Kingdom. They burdened people with obsessive rules that weren't God's rules.

I felt led to expand on this more than some of the other topics, because it's an issue I continue to witness in both the Church and the anti-trafficking movement today. When a survivor is genuinely trying to grow in their relationship with Jesus—whether in a safe home or a new church—and encounters a staff member or leader who operates with a Pharisaical spirit, it can be deeply damaging to their healing journey. The rigid rules, control, manipulation, and self-righteousness often mirror the same dynamics they experienced under their trafficker. What was meant to be a place of safety and restoration can quickly feel unsafe and triggering, causing spiritual confusion and retraumatization. Survivors need compassionate care, not religion cloaked in control.

If you've ever struggled under the weight of religious performance or felt distant from God because of shame or striving, you're not alone. At the end of this book, you'll find a powerful Prayer for Freedom from the Religious Spirit and a practical Tool for Recognizing Religious Mindsets to help you break free and step fully into Kingdom relationship and identity. This is a great resource to discuss and review with ministry teams.

PERSONAL PRAYER PROMPTS

1. God, bring justice.
    I ask You to expose traffickers and bring every hidden thing into the light. Strengthen the systems that are supposed to protect the vulnerable. Let justice be swift, righteous, and redemptive.
2. God, I pray for the healing of traffickers.
    Even though it's hard to imagine, I believe no one is beyond Your reach. I ask You to confront traffickers with Your truth and love. Break through their deception and show them the weight of what they've done. Let conviction lead to repentance and true transformation.
3. Deliver those bound by perversion and lust.
    I lift up every buyer, abuser, and person who fuels the demand for trafficking. Set them free from demonic strongholds of addiction, pornography, and exploitation. I pray for deep deliverance that changes desires and ends cycles of harm.
4. Interrupt the plans of traffickers and buyers.

Lord, I ask You to divinely interrupt the plans of those seeking to harm others. Expose every dark scheme and bring it to ruin. Send confusion into their operations and create divine roadblocks that protect the vulnerable.

5. Let redemption come even to the darkest hearts.
    I may not understand how, but I believe in the power of the cross. I ask You to raise former traffickers and buyers who have turned to You to become testimonies of Your grace and agents of justice and restoration.

6. Help me pray from a place of mercy, not hatred.
    God, when I am tempted to respond with rage or judgment, help me remember that Your justice is perfect and Your mercy is mighty. Let me pray with truth and authority, but also with hope that even those who did evil can be changed by Your love if they repent and turn from their wicked ways.

7. Help me see abuse for what it is.
    If I have ever experienced narcissistic abuse, been groomed, love-bombed, gaslit, or controlled, help me recognize it now. Give me clarity about what really happened so I can stop blaming myself and start healing. I ask you for healing and freedom in Jesus' name.

8. Jesus, what do you want to say to me, show me, or reveal to me? (Wait on the Lord in His presence. Journal what you see, hear, or feel He is revealing to you.)

NOTES

CHAPTER 3

INTERACTING WITH POTENTIAL VICTIMS

When working with potential victims of sex trafficking, it's important to approach every interaction with sensitivity, empathy, and a victim-centered approach. Trauma-informed care should be the guiding principle in all interactions, and this includes prioritizing the victim's safety and well-being, building trust, offering choices, collaborating with them, and empowering them.

To establish a safe and trusting relationship with the victim, service providers should ensure that the victim feels safe and secure. They should also be compassionate, caring, and follow through on their promises to build trust with the victim. Providing options and letting the victim make choices demonstrates that you value their thoughts and feelings and is a key component of trauma-informed care.

This is why it is harmful to force Jesus on a victim who is not ready to explore faith. For the individual, it can feel like you are trying to judge, manipulate, and control them. You can share the gospel with them... But ultimately, it must be their choice. Pressuring a victim or survivor to do anything can make them feel like they can't trust you. They will be watching you, your staff, and your team to see if the Jesus you serve looks attractive to them.

When communicating with potential victims, it's important to stay safe and be aware that the trafficker may be watching or listening. You should speak to them one-on-one and express care and concern, while also being non-judgmental and respectful of their choices. It's crucial to stay positive, patient, and avoid making promises that cannot be kept.

Service providers should also be mindful of not trying to fix or diagnose the victim's trauma, as this can be disempowering and may not be helpful. Instead, they should be active listeners, providing emotional support, and empowering the victim to make decisions about their own healing journey.

To assess whether a person is a victim of sex trafficking, the US Department of State suggests asking specific questions related to their work, freedom of movement, and personal circumstances. These questions can help identify signs of coercion, exploitation, or control, and can inform appropriate interventions.

- Can you leave your job if you want to?
- Can you come and go as you please?

- Have you been hurt or threatened if you tried to leave?
- Has your family been threatened?
- Do you live with your employer?
- Where do you sleep and eat?
- Are you in debt to your employer?
- Do you have your passport/identification? Who has it?

Ultimately, interacting with potential victims of sex trafficking requires compassion, sensitivity, and a trauma-informed approach. By building trust, empowering the victim, and offering support, service providers can help survivors recover and move forward with their lives.

WHY VICTIMS DON'T WANT TO TALK TO YOU

"Building rapport is the first step in interviewing victims in a trauma-informed way. It is critical to keep in mind that a victim's reality is your reality when preparing for and conducting investigative interviews with potential trafficking victims... Law enforcement task force members need to be mindful that human trafficking investigations are purposely victim-centered because the victim supplies the most critical evidence—personal testimony—if there is a trial. However, victims must be stabilized both mentally and physically and must feel safe before investigators can begin in-depth interviews, and service providers and civil attorneys can provide essential support."

—Office for Victims of Crime. (n.d.). Human Trafficking Task Force E-Guide. [Online].

Available: https://www.ovcttac.gov/task-forceguide
[Accessed: March 30, 2023].

Sex trafficking victims may struggle to communicate with service providers for various reasons, and it is essential to understand these reasons to provide effective support and assistance. Some of the reasons that victims may not want to talk include:

1. Trauma: Victims have experienced severe trauma, and talking about it can be incredibly triggering and overwhelming. They may have anxiety or panic attacks just to meet with service providers, unsure of what they will have to relive by talking about the trauma. They may also fear the effects of facing and talking about the trauma.

2. Triggering environment: Some victims may find it difficult to talk in certain locations or environments, especially if something in the room reminds them of their trauma.

3. Feeling judged and misunderstood: Victims may feel judged and misunderstood by service providers, especially if they have had negative experiences in the past.

4. Fear of being a "snitch": Victims may feel like service providers just want information and do not actually care about them or what happens to them after they give the information. They may worry about the consequences of reporting, such as retaliation from their trafficker or the justice system.

5. Lack of safety: Victims may not feel safe around service providers, especially if they have had to provide sex acts for people in the same profession during their trafficking.

6. Fractured memory: Some victims may have suppressed traumatic memories, making it difficult for them to remember details or to acknowledge that something happened.

7. Fear of retaliation: Victims may be terrified that their trafficker will find out they told someone and that there will be severe consequences.

8. Paranoia: Victims may be paranoid that service providers could be working with their trafficker, even in the justice system.

9. Code words: Service providers may use certain words or phrases that trigger victims or remind them of their trauma.

10. Communication style: Service providers may come across as too aggressive, forceful, or lacking compassion, making it difficult for victims to feel comfortable talking.

11. Lack of advocacy: Victims may not have an advocate or trusted person with them to comfort them through the process and stick up for them if they are triggered or mishandled.

12. Broken promises: Service providers may have made promises that they did not follow through on, leading to mistrust and reluctance to talk.

13. Using pet names: Service providers using pet names like "Honey" or "Sweetie" can be a trigger for victims, reminding them of names their traffickers and customers used.

14. Fake safe people: Someone around the victim may be faking that they are a safe person, but they are loyal to the trafficker or cult and will report back.
15. Dissociative identity disorder (DID): If the victim has DID, a protector or cult loyal alter/part may be leading, making it difficult for them to communicate with service providers.
16. Emotional distress: Victims may be having a triggering and emotional day, making it challenging to communicate.
17. Fear of consequences: Victims may be scared that they will get in trouble or lose support if they tell the truth about what is going on.
18. Lack of trust: Victims may not trust service providers due to negative past experiences.
19. Personal choice: Finally, victims may simply not feel like talking or may not be ready to talk about their experiences.

"Trust in the Lord completely, and do not rely on your own opinions. With all your heart, rely on him to guide you, and he will lead you in every decision you make. Become intimate with him in whatever you do, and he will lead you wherever you go. Don't think for a moment that you know it all, for wisdom comes when you adore him with undivided devotion and avoid everything that's wrong. Then you will find the healing refreshment your body and spirit long for." (Proverbs 3:5-8 TPT)

It is crucial to be compassionate, kind, and caring when communicating with victims and survivors of sex trafficking. Service providers should understand that it may take time for victims to open up and that each person's journey is unique. It is important to create a safe and supportive environment and to offer resources and assistance at a pace that is comfortable for the victim. Please make space for this reality during intake processes. For example, do not pressure a survivor to share details of their trafficking experience if they are not ready or do not have adequate support in place to process the emotions that often follow disclosure.

PERSONAL PRAYER PROMPTS

1. Lord, I repent for relying on my own understanding.
   I surrender the need to have all the answers. Teach me to lean fully on Your wisdom and not on my assumptions or urgency.
2. Jesus, give me Your compassion.
   I ask You to fill my heart with the kind of love that sees beneath the surface. Let Your gentleness guide my every word and action.
3. Help me be a safe person, not just a helpful one.
   Show me how to create an environment where others feel emotionally and spiritually safe. Let my presence reflect Your peace.

4. Teach me to honor a survivor's pace.
   Convict me, Holy Spirit, if I start rushing someone else's healing or pressuring them to share.
   Help me meet each person with patience, trust,
   and grace.
5. Let my words carry healing.
   Anoint my speech so that every word I say
   brings comfort, not confusion. Help me be hon-
   est, kind, and clear in every interaction.
6. I pray for those who don't feel safe to speak.
   Surround them with Your presence. Even if they
   cannot express their story yet, let them feel
   seen, heard, and valued.
7. Restore the voices of survivors.
   Bring healing to every silenced heart. I stand
   in faith for the healing and freedom of every
   victim and survivor.
8. Jesus, what do you want to say to me, show
   me or reveal to me? (Wait on the Lord in His
   presence. Journal what you see, hear, or feel
   He is revealing to you.)

NOTES

CHAPTER 4

Sex trafficking victims often experience significant trauma, which can impact them in numerous ways. The effects of trauma are not limited to the spiritual realm, as they can also show up physically, mentally, and emotionally. We need to be aware of how complex trauma affects the whole person—body, soul, and spirit.

The Bible teaches us that we should always seek the wisdom and discernment of Jesus when ministering to others:

"If any of you lacks wisdom, let him ask God, who gives generously to all without reproach, and it will be given him." (James 1:5, ESV)

As we pray and minister to sex trafficking victims, it's important to seek Jesus for discernment on the root issues and not be quick to label their struggles as demonic in nature. For instance, if someone is battling depression, it may not necessarily be caused by a demonic presence but could be due to a hormonal or chemical imbalance. Misdiagnosing their situation may lead to further harm, leaving them feeling more hopeless than before. They leave, feeling demonized by someone they trusted.

In our efforts to help sex trafficking victims and survivors, let us remember that the ultimate goal is to bring them to a place of healing and restoration in Christ. This means we must be fully dependent on Him to do so:

"He heals the brokenhearted and binds up their wounds." (Psalm 147:3, ESV)

"And the peace of God, which surpasses all understanding, will guard your hearts and your minds in Christ Jesus." (Philippians 4:7, ESV)

As we humbly seek God's guidance and trust in His power to heal, we can be effective instruments of His love and compassion, bringing hope and restoration to those who have been deeply wounded by the horrors of sex trafficking. Let's look at trauma from all three angles... Body, Soul, and Spirit.

COMMON QUESTIONS ASKED

- Why don't they leave their trafficker?
- Why do they protect their Pimp?
- Why won't they just say they are a victim?
- Why won't they report their abuse?
- Why do some girls return to their pimp after escape or being rescued?

STOCKHOLM SYNDROME

Stockholm Syndrome, Trauma Bonding, and Complex Trauma are all very real experiences that sex trafficking victims may face. These phenomena can be difficult to understand, but service providers need to have a basic understanding of these concepts to provide appropriate care and support for these survivors.

Stockholm Syndrome is a psychological condition where the victim develops feelings of trust or affection toward their captor. In sex trafficking situations, this may occur when the victim believes that their captor is actually protecting them or helping them in some way. It is important to note that Stockholm Syndrome is not a conscious decision made by the victim, but rather a survival mechanism that their brain uses to cope with the trauma they are experiencing.

TRAUMA BONDING

Trauma Bonding is a phenomenon where the victim develops an emotional attachment to their abuser.

This may occur when the abuser uses emotional manipulation, feigned affection, cultural beliefs about debt, physical and emotional abuse to control and maintain obedience from the victim. Trauma bonding can make it difficult for the victim to leave their situation, as they may believe they are in love with their abuser and may defend them. It is important for service providers to understand that trauma bonding is a survival strategy for victims of abuse and intimidation. Trauma bonding usually blends occasional kindness with threats and abuse.

COMPLEX TRAUMA

Complex Trauma is defined as exposure to multiple, often interrelated forms of traumatic experiences and the difficulties that arise as a result of adapting to or surviving these experiences. Sex trafficking victims often face multiple forms of trauma, including fear, debt bondage, addiction, and physical and emotional abuse. These experiences can lead to a range of mental, emotional, and physical health issues, including anxiety, panic attacks, depression, dissociation (DID), unexplained pain in the body (fibromyalgia), and suicidal thoughts.

Unfortunately, it is not uncommon for victims to find it difficult to leave their traffickers. There are several reasons why this happens, including fear, debt bondage, and addiction.

FEAR

One of the primary reasons why victims find it hard to leave their traffickers is fear. Traffickers often use violence and death threats against the victim and their family members if they try to leave or talk to the police. This can create a sense of terror and helplessness in the victim, making it challenging to escape the situation.

DEBT BONDAGE

Another reason why victims struggle to leave their traffickers is debt bondage. Traffickers create inflated debts that are impossible for the victim to pay off. The victim may believe that they legitimately owe the trafficker and will suffer severe consequences if they fail to pay. This creates a cycle of debt and dependency that can be difficult to break.

ADDICTION / SUBSTANCE ABUSE

Additionally, addiction is often a factor in sex trafficking. It is common for traffickers to use drugs to control their victims, forming deep, long-term dependencies on substances to maintain control. Drugs are often involved in the "breaking in" process of the victim, and the need to make money to support the addiction can also lead to debt bondage. Another cause of substance abuse is numbing the emotional and physical pain of the trauma and exploitation. When the drugs are gone, the trauma memories and night torture intensify.

The reasons why sex trafficking victims find it hard to leave their traffickers are complex and interrelated. Fear, debt bondage, and addiction all play a significant role in perpetuating this heinous crime. It is essential to raise awareness about these issues and provide support and resources to help victims break free from their traffickers and start a new life. Service providers should be aware of the potential for Stockholm Syndrome, Trauma Bonding, and Complex Trauma in sex trafficking survivors and provide appropriate care and support that acknowledges these phenomena. This may include trauma-informed therapy, safety planning, and referral to specialized services that can address the unique needs of trafficking survivors. It is important for service providers to approach these survivors with compassion, empathy, and an understanding of the complex experiences they may have endured.

PRAYER STRATEGIES TO CONSIDER FOR SURVIVORS

- Break Soul Ties with traffickers and buyers
- Renounce vows, judgments, covenants and contracts with traffickers, other victims, buyers and locations
- (Sample Prayer in "Resources" section at the conclusion of this book)
- More training on how to minister to sex trafficking survivors is available at www.TakeFlightSurvivors.org/Academy

TRAUMA, SYMPTOMS, AND BEHAVIORS

Sex trafficking victims endure a range of traumatic experiences that can have long-lasting impact on their physical, emotional, and psychological well-being. These experiences can lead to a complex set of symptoms and behaviors that may persist long after the individual has escaped from the trafficking situation. Here are some of the common effects of sex trafficking trauma:

1. Complex Post-Traumatic Stress Disorder (C-PTSD):
   Survivors of sex trafficking often develop C-PTSD, a condition that arises from prolonged or repeated exposure to traumatic experiences, such as ongoing abuse, captivity, or coercion. Unlike traditional PTSD, which is typically linked to a single traumatic event, C-PTSD reflects the cumulative impact of sustained trauma over time. Symptoms may include persistent emotional dysregulation, deep feelings of shame or guilt, difficulty in trusting others, intrusive flashbacks, nightmares, hypervigilance, dissociation, and a fragmented sense of identity. Survivors may also struggle with chronic fear, relational difficulties, and an ongoing sense of being unsafe—even long after the trauma has ended.
2. Anxiety disorders and panic attacks: Survivors of sex trafficking may also develop anxiety disorders and panic attacks, which can be

triggered by feelings of helplessness, danger, or a sense of impending doom.

3. Avoidance, disorientation, confusion, phobias: Victims of sex trafficking may also experience avoidance, disorientation, confusion, and phobias, which can make it difficult for them to function in daily life.

4. Emotional Triggers and Flashbacks:
    The senses, body, and emotions may react strongly to something associated with past trauma or abuse—such as a sound, smell, phrase, or relational dynamic. These reactions can lead to intense emotional responses or physical sensations that may feel overwhelming or disorienting. This is often referred to as an *emotional flashback*—a sudden and involuntary re-experiencing of the emotional state connected to past trauma, without necessarily recalling specific memories. Unlike visual flashbacks, emotional flashbacks often manifest as deep fear, shame, helplessness, or grief that feels immediate and real, even when there is no current threat.

5. Feeling stuck, spacing out, checking out, not being able to communicate, move, or get up: Survivors may feel trapped, disconnected from themselves and their surroundings, and may struggle to communicate or take action. This is a component of dissociation.

6. Depression, hopelessness, feelings of sadness, sudden or unexplainable crying, a sense of sinking or weighty heaviness: Survivors may

experience depression, feelings of sadness, and a sense of hopelessness that can make it difficult for them to engage in daily activities.

7. Dissociation, suppressed memories, chunks of time missing, denial, memory loss:
Survivors may experience dissociation, suppressed memories, and memory loss as a result of their trauma, which can make it difficult for them to recall important details or events. You will learn more about this later in the book.

8. Dissociative Disorders: Survivors of sex trafficking may develop dissociative disorders, which are characterized by a disconnection between thoughts, feelings, and identity. This can lead to a feeling of detachment from reality.

9. Distrust of Law Enforcement: Survivors may develop a distrust of law enforcement due to being criminalized by them or because their trafficker brainwashed them to fear law enforcement. Unfortunately, several survivors have experienced being raped by crooked law enforcement personnel during their exploitation.

10. Normalization of Exploitation: Survivors may have been trafficked for so long that it becomes their new normal, and they may struggle to function in a healthy routine.

11. Sleeplessness, nightmares, insomnia: Survivors may experience difficulty sleeping or may have nightmares that are related to their trauma.

12. Feeling inferior to others, feeling of being permanently damaged, fear of rejection: Survivors may feel inferior to others, experience a sense

of permanent damage, and fear rejection due to their trauma.

13. Difficulty concentrating: Survivors may struggle to concentrate on daily activities or may have difficulty with memory recall.

14. Self-harm and suicidal ideation: Survivors may engage in self-harm behaviors or experience suicidal ideation due to their trauma. This usually happens when the trauma has not been processed in a healthy way, and there is a strong urge to escape the pain.

15. Sexual problems, including lack of sexual desire or oversexualized behaviors: Survivors may experience sexual problems, such as a lack of sexual desire or an oversexualized behavior, which can be related to their traumatic experiences.

16. Distrust and fear of strangers: Survivors may develop a distrust and fear of strangers due to their traumatic experiences.

17. Anger, aggression, irritability, mood changes: Survivors may experience mood changes, including anger, aggression, and irritability. This especially occurs when they feel judged, trapped, or when they don't have a choice and feel controlled.

18. Isolating behavior: Survivors may engage in isolating behaviors, which can lead to a sense of loneliness and disconnection from others.

19. Changes in appetite or eating disorders.

20. Bathroom-Related Challenges: Survivors may experience difficulties with consistent

bathroom use, including severe constipation or trouble urinating. These issues can stem from trauma to the pelvic region, the body's response to chronic stress, or a history of neglecting basic self-care needs such as adequate hydration. Shame, fear, and dissociation can also contribute to ongoing struggles with bodily awareness and elimination.

21. Satanic Ritual Abuse

THE NEUROBIOLOGY OF TRAUMA

The neurobiology of trauma experienced by sex trafficking victims is complex and multifaceted. It affects various parts of the brain, including the amygdala, hippocampus, and prefrontal cortex. Understanding how trauma affects these brain regions can help service providers offer better care and support to victims.

The amygdala is responsible for processing fear and emotional responses to traumatic events. Victims of sex trafficking often experience intense emotions when recalling their experiences, and service providers should be prepared to offer extra care and support during these moments. For medical professionals, it is important to chart these emotional breakdowns and note them for future reference. This can serve as valid support to victim testimony should the survivor report their trafficking and go to trial to obtain justice.

The hippocampus is responsible for recalling long-term memory. However, sex trafficking victims may struggle to recall details of their experiences due to fragmented or dissociated memory. This can be used to discredit victims in court, but medical professionals can speak to the neurobiology of trauma to validate the fragmented story and provide a better understanding of the impact of trauma on memory recall.

The prefrontal cortex is responsible for decision-making and rational thinking. However, when a victim is being trafficked, this part of the brain may stop functioning effectively. This can lead to difficulty in making decisions and processing the next steps. Victims may feel disconnected and dissociated during sexual trauma, and may engage in sexual acts without giving consent due to fear and the inability to make rational decisions.

Consider getting an expert witness on the neurobiology of trauma or CPTSD to give their expert opinion in court, supporting the validity of the victim's testimony. These professionals can provide important information about the impact of trauma on the brain to help defend victims in court and ensure that their experiences are taken seriously.

Understanding the neurobiology of trauma is crucial for providing effective care and support to sex trafficking victims. Service providers should be prepared to offer extra care and support during emotional breakdowns, validate fragmented memories, and provide important information about the impact of trauma on decision-making and consent.

We should also consider praying for healing miracles in the parts of the brain and nervous system that have been affected by complex trauma... Believing in faith for their brain, mind, heart and emotions to be healed, redeemed, and made new... As if there was never any trauma and restored to God's original design.

PRAYER POINTS

1. Lord, help me understand the unseen battles.
   I ask You to give me eyes to see beyond behavior and into the pain that caused it. Help me remember that trauma rewires the brain and affects the whole person—body, soul, and spirit.
2. I repent for rushing to judgment.
   Forgive me for the times I've assumed a survivor's symptoms were a choice or a spiritual failure. Teach me to respond with wisdom, not accusation; compassion, not conclusions.
3. Give me discernment without assumption.
   Jesus, help me discern the root causes of pain without jumping to labels. Whether it's trauma, spiritual warfare, or physical imbalance—teach me to be Spirit-led, not opinion-driven.
4. Heal what trauma has broken.
   God, I believe You can restore what has been damaged in the brain, heart, and body. I pray for supernatural healing in the minds and nervous systems of survivors—make all things new again.

5. Break the trauma bonds.
   I stand in prayer for those still emotionally tied to their abusers. In Jesus' name, I ask You to break every soul tie, trauma bond, and false loyalty that keeps survivors connected to their traffickers.
6. Strengthen my heart to walk with the wounded. Lord, when trauma symptoms feel messy or overwhelming, give me the grace to stay present and grounded in love. Let me be a steady and safe companion on someone's healing journey.
7. Jesus, what do you want to say to me, show me, or reveal to me? (Wait on the Lord in His presence. Journal what you see, hear, or feel He is revealing to you.)

NOTES

CHAPTER 5

DISSOCIATION

Sex trafficking is a form of trauma that can cause severe dissociation in its victims. Dissociation is a coping mechanism that the brain uses to protect itself from overwhelming or traumatic experiences. In the case of sex trafficking, dissociation can occur in many different ways.

One common form of dissociation that sex trafficking victims experience is depersonalization. This involves feeling detached from one's body, thoughts, and emotions, as if one is observing them from a distance. Victims may feel like they are watching themselves being abused, rather than experiencing the abuse directly. This can help them to feel less pain and distress during the abuse, but it can also lead to a sense of disconnection from their own body, identity, and emotions after the traumatic event(s).

Another form of dissociation that sex trafficking victims may experience is dissociative amnesia. This involves blocking out memories of traumatic experiences, either partially or completely. Victims may have gaps in their memory or may forget entire periods of time. This can make it difficult for them to process and heal from their experiences, as they may not have a complete understanding of what happened to them.

Dissociative identity disorder (DID), formerly known as multiple personality disorder, is another dissociative disorder that can develop as a result of sex trafficking. DID involves the presence of two or more distinct personality states, each with its own way of perceiving, relating to, and thinking about the world. DID can develop as a way of coping with severe and ongoing abuse, as it allows the victim to dissociate from their experiences and create a separate identity to help them cope.

DID is typically diagnosed through clinical assessment using structured interviews, such as the *Structured Clinical Interview for DSM-5 Dissociative Disorders (SCID-D)* or the *Dissociative Experiences Scale (DES)*. However, if an alter or internal part is leading in counseling or assessment sessions, especially one that presents as highly functional, it is highly possible that the survivor may not be accurately diagnosed. Many survivors learn to protect their inner system and may not reveal their dissociative symptoms unless they feel completely safe and understood.

We will explore DID later in this book from a soul-based perspective. It is also important to note that many individuals who are never formally diagnosed with DID still experience the existence of soul parts or internal alters, as described in the Internal Family Systems (IFS) model. Whether clinically diagnosed or not, understanding these internal dynamics is key to the healing process for many survivors of sex trafficking.

It is important to note that not all sex trafficking survivors will experience dissociation, and those who do may experience it in different ways. Additionally, dissociation is not unique to sex trafficking survivors and can occur in people who have experienced other types of trauma as well.

Understanding the various types of dissociation that sex trafficking victims may experience is crucial for service providers working with survivors. It can help them to be patient and compassionate with survivors who may be struggling with dissociation, and to provide appropriate support and resources to help them heal. With the right treatment and support, survivors can recover from dissociation and other trauma-related mental health conditions.

THE WORDS OF SEX TRAFFICKING SURVIVORS WHO EXPERIENCED DISSOCIATION

In a study on The Prostitution and Trafficking of Women and Children in Minnesota, the women eloquently explained how dissociation helped them survive prostitution.

"'If you're having sex with someone you don't want to, you leave.'

'When the johns were sexually assaulting me, I could be in England or somewhere else until they were done.'

'There's times I'd walk around in a space-out because when I stop and think about reality, I break down and can't handle it.'

'[Dissociation is] cutting myself off from my body. I think of it like a game. Then it's [the prostitution] done and over with.'

'It's a way of blocking memories...leading a double life within.'

Several women spoke of learning to dissociate during sexual assaults when they were children,

'I learned how to do that [dissociate] when I was a child being raped.'

Another woman spoke of dissociating when she 'was nine years old and being raped, my mind left my body and was looking down from the ceiling...' Dissociation permits psychological survival, whether the traumatic event(s) are slavery, military combat, incest, or prostitution. Dissociation is an elaborate escape and avoidance strategy in which overwhelming human cruelty results in fragmentation of the mind into different parts of the self that observe, experience, react, as well as those that do not know about the harm. A primary function of dissociation is to handle the overwhelming fear, pain, and to deal with the encounter with systematized cruelty that is experienced during prostitution (and earlier abuse), by splitting that off from the rest of the self."

-Farley, M., Matthews, N., Deer, S., Lopez, G., Stark, C., & Huden, E. (2011). Garden of Truth: The Prostitution and Trafficking of Women and Children in Minnesota.

STATEMENTS DISSOCIATED / FRACTURED SURVIVORS MIGHT MAKE

Disclaimer: The following statements are provided for educational purposes only and are not intended to diagnose dissociative identity disorder (DID) or any other medical or psychological condition. These statements are meant to enhance understanding and sensitivity toward survivors grappling with the aftermath of sex trafficking and/or satanic ritual abuse (explained later in the book) and the direct association with fractured soul parts/alters or dissociation. It is essential for service providers to approach these subjects with care and to seek appropriate professional guidance when necessary. Always defer to the expertise of qualified mental health professionals for diagnostic and treatment purposes.

1. During a traumatic experience, I check out and disconnect.
2. I often feel numb or detached from my own emotions, body, or surroundings when I feel overwhelmed.
3. I can mentally escape when experiencing abuse or when feeling triggered or threatened.

4. I have different voices inside that have opinions about decisions I need to make. These voices feel like me. Sometimes, younger versions of me. This makes it challenging for me to make decisions.

5. I find it hard to establish and maintain healthy relationships due to the emotional distance I struggle with.

6. I often have moments of not feeling like myself.

7. I have huge gaps in my memory; I can't remember what happened. I have difficulty recalling specific details of my trafficking and abuse experiences.

8. I feel disconnected from everything around me.

9. It's like I'm watching my life from the outside.

10. Sometimes, I feel like I'm in a dream or a fog.

11. I have moments where I don't recognize myself in the mirror.

12. I feel like I'm going through the motions but not really present.

13. I can't recall significant events or details from my past.

14. It's like my emotions are blocked or locked away.

15. There are times when I can't control my actions, and it feels like someone else is doing things for me.

16. Sometimes, I feel disconnected from my body, like I'm floating.

17. Sometimes, it's hard to tell if my memories are real or imagined.

18. I experience sudden shifts in my mood or personality.
19. I go into autopilot mode and lose track of time.
20. I have identity confusion; I don't know who I really am.
21. Sometimes, my brain gets foggy, and it's hard to grab onto facts or information. It's challenging to have a conversation with anyone when my brain is foggy.
22. I feel like parts of me are stuck in places where trauma happened to me.
23. Things in my home get moved around, and I have no idea how or why. No one else has access to my apartment. Sometimes, I can't find things that are important to me—later, I discover they were hidden somewhere, but I don't remember doing it.

SCRIPTURES TO CONSIDER ABOUT DISSOCIATION

"The Spirit of the Lord God *is* upon Me, Because the Lord has anointed Me To preach good tidings to the poor; He has sent Me to heal the brokenhearted, to proclaim liberty to the captives, And the opening of the prison to *those who are* bound…" (Isaiah 61:1 NLT)

The Hebrew word for "brokenhearted" in this scripture is "Shabar," which means crushed, fractured, shattered, broken into pieces. So not only does Jesus deliver us from demonic oppression and open prisons (locations where we are stuck and trapped), but he also integrates and heals our broken and fractured souls, minds, and hearts. The Scripture passages and prayer strategies provided in this manual are intended to offer a foundational understanding. These are suggestions to bring before Jesus in prayer for the individual you are working with and ministering to. You must be led by Him.

Please refrain from attempting to facilitate integration for a fractured individual, with soul parts or alters, who has experienced sex trafficking without receiving extensive training, and most importantly, without being commissioned and anointed by Jesus to undertake this work. Forcing integration without the survivor's desire to be integrated and/or without Jesus' guidance can cause significant lifelong damage and harm. I teach strategies for integrative prayer—survivor-led and Jesus-led—in my comprehensive online training available at www.TakeFlightSurvivors.org/Academy.

You don't need to be an expert in this area to help survivors of trafficking. Simply being aware of resources and services for referral is crucial so that these individuals can receive the support they need from those who are specifically called to minister to fractured survivors of trafficking. Always remember to be led by the Lord.

It is important to recognize that fractured soul parts (alters or personalities) are not demons, and

therefore, cannot be cast out. This is why it is essential to follow Jesus' leadership and be guided by the Holy Spirit, seeking wisdom, revelation, and discernment. While fractured soul parts might have demons attached to them, these parts must be treated with love, honor, and forgiveness, and should be acknowledged for their role in helping the individual survive the pain, torture, abuse, and trauma. In this healing process, the individual learns to love and forgive themselves, allowing the true presence of Jesus into the areas where the fractured soul parts have been trapped and compartmentalized.

When ministering to a survivor with fractured soul parts, it is important to offer prayer, comfort, encouragement, or scripture in a way that reaches every part of their being—**without attempting to initiate integration without adequate training**, which should only be facilitated by those trained in safe and appropriate survivor-led methods. A gentle way to begin ministering in prayer is by saying something like, *"I speak to every part of you, in every location and on every timeline..."* Then, continue as the Holy Spirit leads, ensuring that all parts feel seen, valued, and invited to experience the love, truth, and safety of God's presence. This approach honors the complexity of their healing journey without overstepping into territory that requires specialized training.

AWAKEN AND OPEN EVERY PART, INVITING JESUS TO ENTER INTO EVERY PLACE

"Open up, ancient gates! Open up, ancient doors, and let the King of glory enter. Who is the King of glory? The Lord, strong and mighty; the Lord, invincible in battle. Open up, ancient gates! Open up, ancient doors, and let the King of glory enter. Who is the King of glory? The Lord of Heaven's Armies—he is the King of glory." (Psalm 24:7-10 NLT)

This scripture is an approach to invite Jesus into every place within, allowing Him to unlock and open the prisons where these parts are confined and trapped in trauma memories. The ultimate goal is to introduce the true Jesus to every part of the person, sharing the gospel with each aspect of their being so that they can fully experience the healing and redemption found in the finished work of the cross.

In the process of healing sex trafficking survivors who experience dissociation, it is essential to recognize and minister to each distinct part of the individual. Psalm 24:7-10 speaks to the transformative power of embracing the true Jesus in one's life. When addressing the needs of survivors with fractured soul parts, or DID, it is crucial to understand that while some parts of the person might have a strong connection to Jesus, others may not yet trust Him. They may even be completely atheist or against Him. This does not mean that the part is a demon. These parts might still be grappling with the trauma that led to their dissociation, potentially even blaming Jesus for allowing such suffering to occur.

It is common for survivors with fractured soul parts to invest significant time and effort into counseling, prayer, and various therapeutic methods, only to find that their healing remains incomplete. The reason for this lack of progress often lies in the fact that not all parts of the person have been ministered to, as they remain compartmentalized and disconnected from the healing process. This can leave survivors feeling disheartened and struggling to understand why the methods that work for others do not seem to work for them.

The key to lasting freedom and healing for these individuals is to help them encounter the true Jesus in a way that allows for the integration of all parts of their being. Counselors, prayer teams, and ministers must be trained to recognize and address the unique needs of survivors with fractured soul parts or DID, ensuring that they are able to minister to the whole person, rather than just a single aspect of their identity. By facilitating an encounter with Jesus that reaches all fractured parts, lasting freedom and healing can be achieved, allowing survivors to move forward on their journey toward wholeness and restoration. Jesus is the one who heals the broken, fractured heart and soul (Isaiah 61:1). Introducing Him to the parts and personalities of a survivor is the greatest step toward complete healing. He is faithful in completing the work He starts.

"For I am confident of this very thing, that He who began a good work in you will perfect it until the day of Christ Jesus." (Philippians 1:6 NASB)

HIDE MY SOUL IN YOU

"Yahweh my God, I turn aside to hide my soul in you. Save me from all those who pursue and persecute me." (Psalms 7:1 TPT)

"O Lord my God, in you do I take refuge; save me from all my pursuers and deliver me, lest like a lion they tear my soul apart, rending it in pieces, with none to deliver." (Psalm 7:1-2 ESV)

Pray that the survivor's soul would be hidden in the Lord. Safety from people who seek to hurt and exploit their vulnerabilities is imperative for healing, breakthrough, and growth.

PERSONAL PRAYER PROMPTS

1. Jesus, I invite You into every part of me.
   I open the doors of my heart, soul, and mind—every timeline, every memory, and every compartmentalized place. Come, King of Glory. Shine Your light into the areas I've hidden, the parts I didn't even know needed You.
2. Teach me to love every part of myself.
   Even the parts of my life that I've avoided, judged, or subconsciously ignored. Help me to welcome them with grace. Thank You for sustaining me through the painful moments in my life. Jesus, I invite you to heal me.

3. Lord, help me understand dissociation with compassion.
   Whether I've experienced it or not, give me eyes to see and a heart to understand the depth of pain that causes someone to disconnect from themselves. Teach me to walk gently, never assuming or minimizing what I don't fully understand.
4. Jesus, I lift up every survivor whose soul has been fractured by trauma.
   I ask You to surround them with Your presence, safety, and comfort. Speak peace to the parts of them that are afraid, lost, or trapped. Let them know they are not alone, and that You are able to restore what was shattered.
5. Restore the minds and memories of survivors.
   For every survivor living with dissociation, memory loss, fog, or identity confusion—I ask for miraculous healing. Bring order where there has been chaos, and light, where there has been darkness. Rewire what trauma has broken.
6. Jesus, teach me how You see dissociation.
   Give me Your heart and perspective on this survival response. Show me how You minister to the ones who feel fragmented. Let me carry Your love, language, and wisdom when walking alongside those who live with this reality.
7. Jesus, minister to every fractured soul.
   I pray for every survivor still living with dissociation. Surround them with trained, compassionate people. Let them feel safe enough to

begin healing. Show them that You are not like the ones who hurt them—and that You will never leave.

8. Jesus, what do you want to say to me, show me, or reveal to me? (Wait on the Lord in His presence. Journal what you see, hear, or feel He is revealing to you.)

NOTES

CHAPTER 6

"Afterward, Simeon, a Jewish religious leader, asked Jesus to his home for dinner. Jesus accepted the invitation. When he went to Simeon's home, he took his place at the table.

In the neighborhood, there was an immoral woman of the streets, known to all to be a prostitute. When she heard that Jesus was at Simeon's house, she took an exquisite flask made from alabaster, filled it with the most expensive perfume, went right into the home of the Jewish religious leader, and in front of all the guests, she knelt at the feet of Jesus. Broken and weeping, she covered his feet with the tears that fell from her face. She kept crying and drying his feet with her long hair. Over and over, she kissed Jesus' feet. Then, as an act of worship, she opened her flask and anointed his feet with her costly perfume.

When Simeon saw what was happening, **he thought**, "This man can't be a true prophet. If he were really a prophet, he would know what kind of sinful woman is touching him."

Jesus said, "Simeon, I have a word for you."

"Go ahead, Teacher. I want to hear it," he answered. "It's a story about two men who were deeply in debt. One owed the bank one hundred thousand dollars, and the other only owed ten thousand dollars. When it was obvious that neither of them would be able to repay their debts, the kind banker graciously wrote off the debts and forgave them all that they owed. Tell me, Simeon, which of the two debtors would be more thankful? Which one would love the banker most?"

Simeon answered, "I suppose it would be the one with the greater debt forgiven."

"You're right," Jesus agreed. Then he spoke to Simeon about the woman still weeping at his feet.

"Do you see this woman kneeling here? She is doing for me what you didn't bother to do. When I entered your home as your guest, you didn't think about offering me water to wash the dust off my feet. Yet she came into your home and washed my feet with her many tears and then dried my feet with her hair. You didn't even welcome me into your home with the customary kiss of greeting, but from the moment I came in, she has not stopped kissing my feet. You didn't take the time to anoint my head with fragrant oil, but she anointed my head and feet with the finest perfume. She has been forgiven of all her many sins. This is why she has shown me such extravagant love. But those who assume they have very little to be forgiven will love me very little."

Then Jesus said to the woman at his feet, "All your sins are forgiven."

All the dinner guests said among themselves, "Who is the one who can even forgive sins?"

Then Jesus said to the woman, "Your faith in me has given you life. Now you may leave and walk in the ways of peace." (Luke 7:36-50 TPT)

This scripture tells the story of a woman who had a reputation for being a known prostitute, who came to Jesus while he was dining at a Pharisee's house. The Pharisee, Simeon, was critical of Jesus allowing this woman to touch him and expressed his negative thoughts toward her. But Jesus defended her and honored her openly in front of everyone, rebuking Simeon for his judgmental thoughts toward her.

This story illustrates Jesus' deep compassion for people who were marginalized and oppressed, particularly women who were considered outcasts in society. Jesus saw beyond the woman's past and acknowledged her worth as a person made in the image of God. He did not allow the religious leader's negative thoughts to define her or diminish her value. It's so interesting that Simeon didn't even speak those things out loud. Jesus knew his thoughts and rebuked him openly in his own house and in front of all the guests.

As followers of Jesus, we are called to carry the same compassion and desire to defend people coming out of the darkness of the sex industry. We are called to see beyond people's past mistakes and recognize their inherent value and dignity. We are called to stand up for those who are oppressed and marginalized, who have been victims of abuse and exploitation.

Countless victims and survivors are still struggling to escape the bondage of the sex industry, and they need advocates who will defend and honor them. As we follow Jesus' example, we can bring hope and healing to those who have been wounded by the darkness of this world. Let us pray that God would give us the courage and compassion to defend those who are vulnerable and oppressed, and that we would be a light in the darkness for those who need to know God's love and grace.

Pure intimacy with Jesus overrides trauma, sexual assault, and all forms of demonic perversion.

COMPASSION METER

As Christians, we are called to love one another and show compassion to those who are hurting. This includes victims of sex trafficking, who have often experienced unimaginable trauma and suffering. In scripture, when Jesus was moved with compassion, that's when many miracles happened... Healing, deliverance, signs, and wonders. Miracles are a byproduct of moving in compassion, radical obedience and faith.

Compassion is not just a feeling, but an action. It means actively seeking out ways to help and support those who are in need. This can include providing practical assistance such as food, shelter, and medical care, as well as emotional and spiritual support. However, it is important to recognize that caring for sex trafficking victims can be a challenging and emotionally draining task. It is easy to become overwhelmed and lose compassion in the face of such immense suffering. This is why it is crucial to regularly check our compassion meter and take steps of self-care to prevent burnout.

One way to do this is through prayer and seeking God's guidance and strength. We can also lean on our fellow team members and supporters for support and encouragement. Taking regular breaks and self-care measures can also help to recharge our compassion meter and prevent burnout.

Ultimately, the goal of showing compassion to sex trafficking victims is not just to bring about physical and emotional healing, but also to share the love and hope of Christ with them. By demonstrating compassion and kindness toward these vulnerable individuals, we can point them toward the ultimate source of healing and redemption, Jesus Christ.

PERSONAL PRAYER PROMPTS

1. Jesus, give me Your heart for the ones the world rejects. Help me see survivors of exploitation and of the sex industry the way You do—with compassion, honor, and deep understanding.

Teach me to see their worth as Your beloved sons and daughters.

2. Forgive me for judging what I don't understand. If I've ever looked down on someone because of their past, even in my thoughts, I repent. I renounce pride. I ask You to remove every trace of pride and replace it with humility and love.

3. I repent for agreeing with legalism and the religious spirit.

    Jesus, I renounce every judgmental thought, religious lie, and performance-based mindset I've believed. I break agreement with every legalistic voice that told me, or others, that we had to earn holiness and Your love. In Jesus' name, I repent and renounce the religious, legalistic spirit and to go along with all legalistic programming in Jesus' name. I receive Your grace, truth, and freedom.

4. Teach me how to defend and honor survivors. When others stay silent or cast judgment, give me the courage to speak up. Let me be someone who stands between survivors and shame, pointing always to Your love and restoration.

5. Reignite my compassion when I feel numb or overwhelmed.

    If I've grown weary or disconnected from the deep suffering survivors face, renew my heart. Fill me again with compassion that moves me to action, prayer, and advocacy.

6. Let my intimacy with You override every form of sexual trauma or perversion.

I declare that Your love is greater than any trauma, or perversion that I've experienced or engaged in. I renounce lust, sexual perversion, fornication, etc. in Jesus' name. If I've watched pornography, Jesus, I repent now. *(If yes, read the Soul Tie Prayer in Resources Section.)* Purify every part of me. Let the healing power of Your presence restore everything the enemy tried to destroy. I receive your forgiveness and righteousness made available to me through the finished work of the cross.

7. Jesus, what do you want to say to me, show me or reveal to me? (Wait on the Lord in His presence. Journal what you see, hear, or feel He is revealing to you.)

NOTES

PART TWO: SATANIC RITUAL ABUSE / OCCULT TRAFFICKING

CHAPTER 7

INTRODUCTION TO SATANIC RITUAL ABUSE (SRA), OCCULT CRIMES, MIND CONTROL, AND SEX TRAFFICKING

A NOTE BEFORE YOU BEGIN

This section addresses deeply challenging and heavy topics. While the content may be difficult to process, it is essential for a comprehensive understanding of the realities many survivors face. I encourage you to read through with the knowledge that this chapter concludes on a note of empowerment and hope. You will find encouragement, prayer points, and the reminder that, through Christ Jesus, we have greater authority and victory over darkness.

"The reason the Son of God was revealed was to undo and destroy the works of the devil." -1 John 3:8 TPT

"Now you understand that I have imparted to you all my authority to trample over his Kingdom. You will trample upon every demon before you and overcome every power Satan possesses. Absolutely nothing will be able to harm you as you walk in this authority." -Luke 10:19 TPT

"When a strong man, with many weapons, guards his palace, his possessions are safe. But when one stronger than he comes to attack and overpower him, the stronger one will empty the arsenal in which he trusted. The conqueror will ransack his kingdom and distribute all the spoils of victory. Whoever is not on my side is against me, and whoever does not gather the spoils with me will be forever scattered." -Luke 11:21-23 TPT

LET'S BEGIN

"~20% of the survivors of sex trafficking who seek help with escape have satanic ritual abuse in their exploitation history." -Rescue America

We are living in a prophetic moment, one that mirrors the shift our nation experienced about two decades ago when we first began to define and address sex trafficking. In 2000, the United States passed the Trafficking Victims Protection Act (TVPA), the first comprehensive federal law to combat human trafficking, including sex trafficking. At the time, survivors were misidentified as criminals and labeled as prostitutes, addicts, or runaways. There were no federal protections for victims, no reliable data, and few systems in place to prosecute traffickers and perpetrators. This is because the right questions weren't being asked. It took courageous survivors and abolitionists to shift the narrative and awaken the nation.

Today, we are in a similar wave of awakening... this time concerning Satanic Ritual Abuse (SRA). Just as it once was with sex trafficking, most people are only now beginning to understand the realities of SRA and its deep ties to trafficking networks. In 2025, Utah passed House Bill 66, known as the "Ritual Abuse Amendments," officially recognizing ritual abuse of a child as a second-degree felony. The law defines specific acts—including animal sacrifice, ingestion of bodily fluids, mock ceremonies, and spiritual manipulation—as components of ritual abuse. It also mandates specialized training for law enforcement to help identify indicators of ritual abuse in sexual assault investigations. This groundbreaking legislation represents the first of its kind in the U.S., and it signals a growing national shift toward awareness, truth, accountability, and justice for survivors. Service providers who work with sex trafficking victims must understand Satanic Ritual Abuse and know how to serve these individuals without judgment and with quality trauma-informed survivor care.

"He is the revealer of profound and hidden mysteries. He knows all hidden things, for he is light, and darkness is no obstacle to him." — Daniel 2:22 (TPT)

KEY TERMS: UNDERSTANDING THE LANGUAGE OF SRA

Before we explore the complex and often hidden realities of Satanic Ritual Abuse (SRA), it's important to define a few core terms. These brief explanations will help ground your understanding as we move through survivor testimonies, historical research, biblical insight, and spiritual principles.

SPIRITUAL ABUSE

Spiritual abuse is the misuse of religious authority, doctrine, or practices to control, manipulate, shame, or harm others. It often involves physical or sexual abuse that is justified or excused through distorted interpretations of scripture, religious roles, or divine will. This type of abuse may occur in churches, religious institutions, or other faith-based communities, where leaders or members use spiritual beliefs to silence victims, demand submission, sexually abuse, or coerce obedience. Survivors of spiritual abuse may struggle with deep confusion, mistrust of religious environments, and feelings of shame, guilt, or fear tied to their faith.

SATANIC RITUAL ABUSE (SRA)

Satanic Ritual Abuse is a highly organized and spiritually charged form of abuse that involves sexual, physical, psychological, and spiritual trauma. It is typically carried out by cults or groups that worship Satan or demonic entities. SRA often includes rituals, sacrifices, blood covenants, and programming methods designed to fracture the soul and create dissociated "parts" or alternate personalities. Many SRA survivors are also victims of familial and sex trafficking networks, where the abuse begins in early childhood and continues through ritual calendars and cult systems of control.

OCCULT CRIMES

Occult crimes refer to criminal acts—such as sexual abuse, human trafficking, ritual sacrifice, or torture—committed in the context of occult practices. These crimes are often committed by individuals or groups who believe in esoteric, mystical, or satanic power structures, including some secret societies, witchcraft covens, and Satanic cults. Occult crimes often involve symbols, rituals, coded language, spiritual contracts, and desecration of the human body for perceived supernatural gain.

MIND CONTROL PROGRAMMING

Mind control programming is the systematic use of trauma, repetition, and spiritual manipulation to fracture the human mind and create dissociated identities (also called "alters" or parts). These parts are then programmed with specific codes, phrases, roles, or triggers to ensure obedience and secrecy. This method, often beginning in early childhood, may include extreme torture, hypnosis, drugs, rituals, and sexual abuse. Many survivors of SRA report programming that mirrors known government projects like MK Ultra, which used similar methods to create highly controlled individuals for exploitation and covert operations.

HISTORICAL ROOTS AND MODERN EXPRESSIONS

Satanic Ritual Abuse (SRA) is a controversial and often misunderstood topic, but it is a real phenomenon that has affected many individuals. It is a form of extreme abuse involving physical, sexual, spiritual, and emotional trauma, often in the context of a cult or group that worships Satan or other malevolent entities.

Many victims report being abused and trafficked by individuals in religious cults, Satanism, witchcraft groups, and occult-based secret societies. Not all members of these religious groups are involved in trafficking; however, survivors frequently identify high-ranking members of these cults as perpetrators.

Lower-level participants may or may not be aware of the trafficking activities.

To understand the most hidden and complex forms of sex trafficking, it is essential to understand SRA. Whether or not someone believes these testimonies, the survivors' realities must be honored. Within their stories may lie critical intelligence that could dismantle trafficking networks.

It's important to recognize that SRA involves ancient patterns of ritual abuse that continue in modern times. Notorious gangs and cartels, such as MS-13 and various satanic-affiliated criminal networks, are known to engage in human sacrifices and ritual abuse as part of their exploitation of both minors and adults. These groups perpetuate the same horrific practices described throughout history, underscoring that the battle against ritual abuse and occult crimes is not confined to the past. Understanding these modern expressions of evil is crucial for those committed to bringing healing and freedom to survivors today.

SRA TRAFFICKING IN THE BIBLE: EXPOSING THE ANCIENT ROOTS OF RITUAL ABUSE AND OCCULT CRIMES

Satanic Ritual Abuse (SRA) is not a new phenomenon. It is an ancient practice, seen throughout both biblical history and world cultures, cloaked under the names of idolatry, fertility worship, cult prostitution, and temple rituals. The Bible does not shy away from exposing these evil systems, and neither should we.

TERMINOLOGY IN ANCIENT CULTIC SYSTEMS

Terms used throughout history for ritualized sex slaves include:

- Temple Prostitute
- Shrine Prostitute
- Sacred Prostitute
- Cult Prostitute
- Hebrew terms: Qadistu, Qedesha, Kedeshah (used for both males and females)

These individuals, many of them children, were dedicated to pagan gods (principalities and demons) by their fathers or temple authorities. They were forced to serve in temple sex rituals, believed to ensure agricultural and economic prosperity. The "worship" was actually demonic ritual abuse, involving sexual exploitation, soul bondage, and spiritual defilement.

"It can be defined narrowly as union with a prostitute... sanctioned by the wardens of a deity... in such cases, the prostitute had semi-official status as a cult functionary... The prostitutes would be slaves owned by the temple." — Journal of the Evangelical Theological Society, 42.3 (1999)

In other words, many so-called "sacred" prostitutes were trafficked victims, abused in the name of pagan false gods like Baal, Molech, Asherah, and Ishtar.

HISTORICAL CONFIRMATION OF SRA SYSTEMS

- Greek historian Strabo (64 BC–AD 21) wrote about the Temple of Aphrodite in Corinth, which had over 1,000 temple-slaves—both men and women—dedicated to the goddess for ritual sex. "The temple of Aphrodite was so rich that it owned more than a thousand temple-slaves, courtesans (hetairai), whom both women and men had dedicated to the goddess…"— Strabo, Geography
- Herodotus, the "father of history," confirmed that even fathers consecrated their daughters to be used in temple prostitution (sex trafficking), often as a rite of passage.
- Scholar Everett Ferguson writes: "Prostitution became a part of religious rites at certain temples… there were one thousand 'sacred prostitutes' at the temple of Aphrodite at Corinth." — Backgrounds of Early Christianity
- Van der Toorn adds, "When speaking of cultic prostitution, scholars normally refer to religiously legitimated intercourse… The money or the goods received went to the temple funds." — Anchor Bible Dictionary (ABD 5.510)

This is sex trafficking. The victims were forced to do ritual sex acts in obedience to pagan false gods, demons, while giving the money to the pagan temples.

SCRIPTURAL EVIDENCE OF RITUAL ABUSE AND CULT PROSTITUTION

The Bible directly references and condemns these evil practices:

Deuteronomy 23:18 (NLT)

"When you are bringing an offering to fulfill a vow, you must not bring to the house of the Lord your God any offering from the earnings of a prostitute, whether a man or a woman, for both are detestable to the Lord your God."

This shows that male and female prostitution tied to religious systems was happening in the biblical era, and God considered it detestable. It was so widespread that God had to bring clear instruction, warning His people not to approach Him with offerings derived from ritual sex acts; acts that were not only abusive but rooted in demonic worship.

Hosea 4:14 (NLT)

"But why should I punish them for their prostitution and adultery? For your men are doing the same thing, sinning with whores and shrine prostitutes. O foolish people! You refuse to understand, so you will be destroyed."

Men of Israel were complicit, participating in shrine prostitution and perpetuating the abuse cycle. God was grieved, not just by the sin, but by the refusal to understand and repent.

Isaiah 57:3–9 (NLT)

This intense prophetic rebuke outlines the depth of Israel's idolatrous rituals—including child sacrifice and spiritual adultery:

"You sacrifice your children down in the valleys... You have committed adultery on every high mountain... You have gone to Molech with olive oil and many perfumes, sending your agents far and wide, even to the world of the dead."

Genesis 38

The story of Tamar and Judah shows that shrine prostitution was known and culturally understood, as Judah mistook Tamar for a shrine prostitute (kedeshah) and offered payment without hesitation.

THE SPIRITUAL CONSEQUENCES OF SEXUAL RITUALS

The Bible also warns of the deep spiritual effects of sexual sin, especially when tied to occult systems:

"Don't you realize that if a man joins himself to a prostitute, he becomes one body with her? ... Run from sexual sin! No other sin so clearly affects the body as this one does." 1 Corinthians 6:16–18 (NLT)

Sexual union creates soul ties and opens spiritual access points, gateways that are intentionally exploited in Satanic rituals. This is why Satanic Ritual Abuse is not merely physical abuse; it is deep spiritual bondage. Fornication enables the rapid spread of demonic influence, and within the context of rituals, it becomes a powerful tool, a highway of satanic transfer. Orgasms, in the spirit realm, function as spiritual covenants, allowing the full exchange of demonic attachments, soul programming, and trauma between individuals. This may be one reason why sex trafficking and ritual abuse are so pervasive, because sexual acts are one of the most effective and direct ways for Satan to spread darkness, control, and carry out his destructive agenda.

WHAT DOES THIS MEAN FOR US TODAY?

Satanic Ritual Abuse may be cloaked in modern language and hidden within complex systems, but its core methods and demonic agenda remain the same. What once took place in public temples now operates in secret through underground trafficking networks. Ancient pagan leaders have been replaced by covert operatives within secret societies and high-level systems of power. The enemy's goal has not changed: to dedicate victims to demonic entities, program and control their minds, perform ritual sex acts, and exploit them for money, influence, and spiritual power—all in service to Satan's dark agenda.

But just as this evil has ancient roots, so does our authority. We are not powerless. Jesus came to destroy the works of the devil (1 John 3:8), and He has given us authority to cast out demons, heal the brokenhearted, and set the captives free (Luke 10:19, Isaiah 61:1).

DISSOCIATION, TRAUMA, AND PROGRAMMING

One of the most well-documented and disturbing examples of mind control experimentation is MK Ultra, a covert U.S. government program operated by the CIA from the 1950s through the 1970s. Declassified documents and survivor testimonies reveal that MK Ultra involved non-consensual experiments on civilians, including the use of trauma, drugs, hypnosis, isolation, and electroshock to manipulate and fracture the human mind. While the program was officially shut down, its tactics did not disappear; they evolved. Many survivors of Satanic Ritual Abuse (SRA) describe nearly identical methods of programming and psychological torture, often beginning in early childhood. These survivors report being subjected to intense trauma designed to break down their sense of identity and create dissociated parts (also called "alters") that could be programmed to obey commands without conscious awareness.

MK Ultra programming is closely related to another commonly known government initiative: Operation Paperclip. After World War II, the United States secretly recruited Nazi scientists, including those who had conducted horrific mind control and medical experiments under Adolf Hitler's regime. These individuals were brought into the U.S. through Operation Paperclip to continue their research within government agencies, including the CIA. Many of the techniques used in MK Ultra such as trauma-based conditioning, hypnosis, drug experimentation, and dissociative programming, are directly linked to the psychological torture and experimentation carried out in Nazi concentration camps. This transfer of knowledge laid the foundation for modern mind control programs, blending scientific manipulation with spiritual and psychological abuse.

Mainstream culture often glorifies and sensationalizes these themes through science fiction, referencing it in films with super soldier themes or characters under government control. However, these depictions are based on chilling truths. For real survivors, these aren't storylines, they're lived experiences. The pain is not symbolic. The programming is real. The spiritual implications are very complex and multifaceted.

Service providers, advocates, and ministry leaders must understand the sophisticated and deeply spiritual tactics used by occult traffickers and Satanic Ritual Abuse (SRA) networks to brainwash, control, and spiritually enslave their victims.

One of the most common and sinister methods used is known as "programming" or "conditioning." This involves the repeated use of scripts, stories, chants, and curses spoken over a victim while they are being sexually, physically, emotionally, and spiritually tortured. The goal of this systematic abuse is to cause the victim's mind to dissociate and fracture, creating multiple alter personalities (or "parts") that can be more easily manipulated, assigned roles, and controlled.

In these rituals, trigger codes (specific words, phrases, sounds, and names) are drilled into the fractured mind under extreme duress. Victims are often forced to obey these codes without hesitation. If they disobey or fail to respond, they are subjected to further torture, punishment, or threats against their lives or the lives of others they care about. This instills deep-rooted fear and creates a psychological and spiritual prison that can persist for years.

In addition to spoken code words, symbols, and colors play a major role in programming. Just like code words, they are intentionally used to trigger specific alters, enforce obedience, or reactivate traumatic memories. A victim may be forced to sit in a purple room, for example, while being shown programming videos filled with occult symbols, coded language, and subliminal messages. These carefully curated environments are designed to overwhelm the senses, break down natural resistance, and program the fractured soul to comply. That color then becomes psychologically anchored to the specific trauma and programming experience, making it a powerful tool for future control. When paired with coded instructions, the color alone can trigger compliance from the victim—often without conscious awareness—due to the deep associations formed during the original abuse.

The goal of the programmer is not simply behavioral control; it is spiritual domination. Under torture, the victim is coerced into giving an agreement, permission, or "yes" under extreme duress. This forced consent becomes a legal loophole in the spirit realm, permitting demonic entities to attach to one or more of the fractured soul parts. These parts, now dissociated and enslaved, may become what the occult refers to as "mind control slaves," programmed to perform specific tasks, respond to triggers, or carry out rituals.

Code words, symbols, colors, and even certain music, objects, or smells can be used to access specific alters, assign titles or functions within the cult, or trigger behaviors such as self-harm, dissociation, or returning to the abuser. This makes everyday environments full of potential landmines for survivors. Especially if they have not yet begun the deprogramming, deliverance/freedom, and healing process.

If programming details ever emerge in a conversation or session, it is important not to repeat or share those codes with anyone, including well-meaning individuals. Even unintentional exposure to a trigger word or symbol could re-traumatize the survivor or cause an involuntary reaction that leads to harm.

"Ritualistic child abuse is the most hideous of all child abuse. The basic objective is premeditated—to systematically and methodically torture and terrorize children until they are forced to dissociate. The torture is not a consequence of the loss of temper, but the execution of well-planned, well-thought-out rituals often performed by close relatives. The only escape for the children is to dissociate. They develop a new personality to enable them to endure various forms of abuse. When the episode is over, the core personality is again in control, and the individual is not conscious of what happened.

Dissociation also serves the purposes of the occult because the children have no day-to-day memory of the atrocities. They go through adolescence and early adulthood with no active memory of what is taking place. Oftentimes, they continue in rituals through their teens and early twenties, unaware of their involvement."

-Glenn Leroy Pace, General authority of the Church of Jesus Christ of Latter-day Saints; Glenn Pace Memo Interview of 60 SRA Survivors

It is important to note that the creation of soul parts (alters) in SRA is not limited to sex trafficking victims. While some victims may have been specifically programmed to sexually service clients, others may have been programmed for other purposes within the cult, such as carrying out rituals, drug trafficking, violence, or performing other tasks. Additionally, not all victims of SRA are diagnosed with DID, and not all people with DID have a history of SRA.

When interacting with, interviewing, or counseling victims of SRA, it is crucial to understand that their alters and programming were designed to protect the cult and its members. Building trust with these individuals requires compassion, kindness, patience, and consistency, and it may take time to establish a rapport that allows them to share their experiences.

It is also important to ensure that victims of SRA have access to trauma-informed counseling that specializes in treating DID, sex trafficking, and ritual abuse. These individuals require a lot of support, and it is essential to work with trained professionals who understand the complexities of their experiences and can provide appropriate care.

To religious or spiritual communities, it is crucial to understand that the alters created in SRA are not demons, and it is harmful to demonize individuals with DID or fractured soul parts. These individuals require love, forgiveness, and a safe environment to begin the healing process. With compassion and gentleness, it is possible to help these individuals integrate their fractured souls and find healing from their trauma.

The good news is that deprogramming is possible, and healing can happen through trauma-informed care, prayer, inner healing, deliverance, and safe community. Jesus Christ came to set the captives free, and no soul part is too fractured, and no programming too deep, for Him to restore.

"He has sent me to bind up the brokenhearted, to proclaim freedom for the captives and release from darkness for the prisoners." — Isaiah 61:1 (NIV)

With compassion, patience, and the leading of the Holy Spirit, survivors can be set free from these systems of control and fully restored to the identity God originally intended for them. Jesus is more powerful than SRA, and what He did on the cross is enough to deprogram, deliver, and heal!

RITUAL MARKS, SYMBOLS, AND OCCULT FRAMEWORKS

For many SRA victims, the torture and occult rituals start while in the womb because SRA is often "familial trafficking" due to the significance of generational lines. Satanists include their semen and bodily fluids in baby bottles and start the perverse programming and sexual abuse when the victim is a newborn. For SRA victims who have multiple high-up roles forced on them by the cult... There is a very calculated track of rituals, holidays, and events that takes place over the course of their lives. For some, sexual marriage to their father and Satan happens at age 12.

There is an SRA occult calendar for rituals with victims. Satanists are very methodical, patterned, and legalistic. SRA and occult traffickers use the calendar to do rituals and torture. It tells them what kind of sacrifices to make and who should be involved. SRA survivors generally feel very triggered leading up to ritual dates due to compacted and layered trauma on the same day annually. The victim's birthday is a very traumatic experience as well.

A common ritual includes the Satanist biting a piece of the female victim's clitoris as a way to mark and claim them as their property. Other Satanists know that if a victim has a chunk of their clitoris missing, that victim has already been claimed, and they are not allowed to "own" them, only abuse them. This is important for medical professionals to know when conducting a SANE exam and rape kit. If this is identified, then the patient is likely a SRA Trafficking Victim and is a part of an occult network. Cult members will try to find them, and they may have a tracking device implanted (explained below).

KABALLAH TREE

Many Satanic Ritual Abuse (SRA) Cults, Secret Societies, and Witches use the Kabbalah Tree for rituals and curses on victims. They believe it is a pathway and roadmap to the highest spiritual powers in the universe. The Occult Trafficker "sets out to conquer the universe," thereby requiring entry into the "darkest levels of the mind." To succeed, he or she must become master of everything in the universe—evil as well as good, cruelty as well as mercy, pain as well as pleasure (Cavendish, 1967:3). The more trauma these trafficker occult leaders, witchcraft covens and groups can inflict upon victims by engaging with the points on the Kabbalah Tree, the more powerful they believe that they become. Their beliefs and goals are to intentionally fracture the victim, creating parts/

personalities for different roles in the cult that are surrendered to specific demons and geographical territories.

Sex Trafficking Victims of SRA networks may have experienced torture, burns, bruises, tattoos, cuts, and/or scars, illegal surgeries, or restraints in patterns on their bodies. Specifically, on what the cult believes to be spiritual gateways for internal and universal structures in the soul and spirit realm. If patterned marks on the body of a victim are identified, please don't touch the victim in these places. Codes for hypnosis, curses, brainwashing, and mind control are connected with these areas of the body. They are very triggering to the victim.

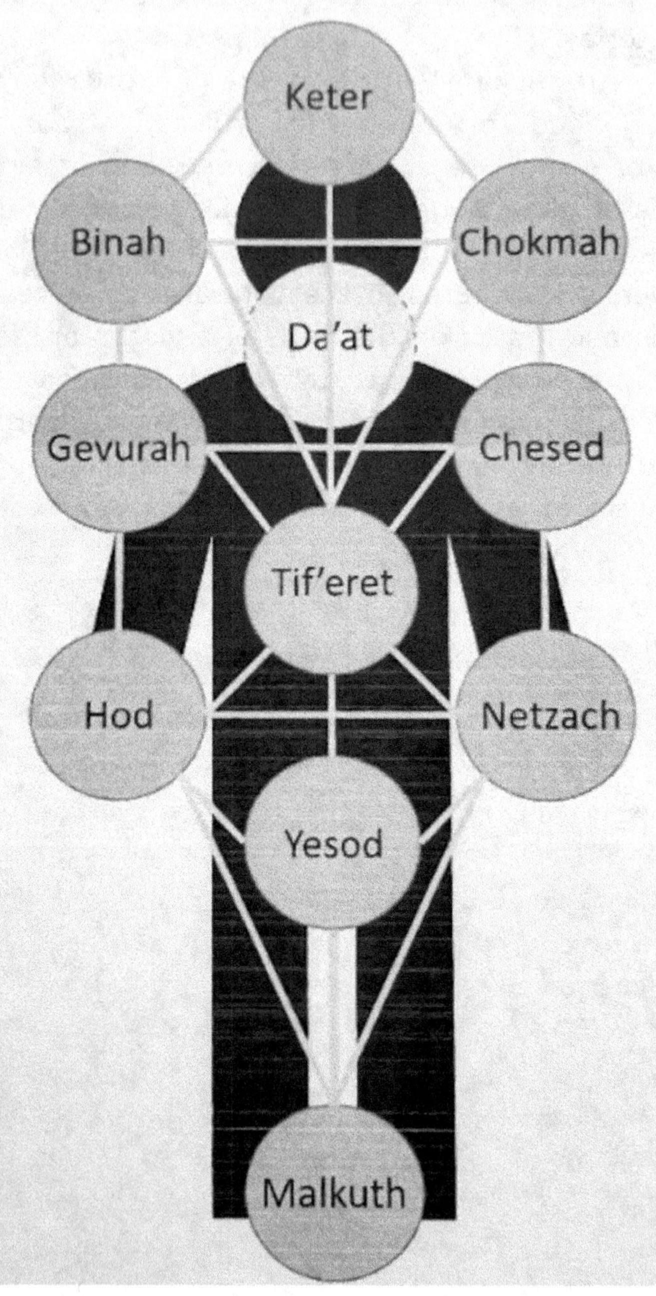

Photo By Dan Duval, Bride Ministries International

ONGOING RISK AND SPIRITUAL HARASSMENT

Many survivors are stalked or harassed after escape. Cults work to retrieve those who held high roles within their systems, especially if the survivor has information that could expose high-level perpetrators. This stalking may involve physical tracking, cyberstalking, impersonation, spiritual attacks, or even implanted tracking devices. The risk increases around occult calendar dates.

Survivors may also describe spiritual harassment, such as demonic dreams, astral assaults in the spirit realm (explained in the next section), or recurring symbolic contact (like text messages with code words or images to program and trigger trauma memories). These experiences are real and debilitating, and care teams must take them seriously.

WHY SURVIVORS AREN'T BELIEVED

Sadly, there are still those within the anti-trafficking movement who choose not to believe the testimonies of survivors who have endured satanic ritual abuse (SRA) and programming during their trafficking. This disbelief often stems from a long-standing campaign, known as the 'Satanic Panic,' which was originally orchestrated to discredit and silence the voices of SRA and mind control survivors. This campaign leveraged media and even government reports to portray survivors as suffering from a mental health psychosis rather than acknowledging the reality of their trauma.

Sociologist Michael Salter has written extensively on this issue, noting that:

> "Organized abuse is not only a form of violence but also a form of knowledge suppression, where the production of ignorance is a deliberate strategy employed by perpetrators to evade detection and accountability." — Michael Salter, The Ant epistemology of Organized Abuse

In faith-based settings, this disbelief can be further compounded by theological differences. Some denominations do not believe in the active presence of the Holy Spirit or the reality of the spiritual realm today, despite these things being evident in scripture. This limited perspective makes it difficult for them to comprehend the profound spiritual and psychological impacts of SRA, leading them to dismiss or misunderstand survivors' experiences.

This lack of belief and understanding is not just a theological issue; it has real consequences for survivors seeking healing. When survivors bravely share their stories only to be met with skepticism, dismissal, and a "mental health psychosis," it compounds their trauma and erodes their trust. Such a response is deeply grieving and harmful. If service providers cannot acknowledge the world history, biblical history, and current realities of SRA occult trafficking, they risk causing further damage to those they aim to help.

This dynamic mirrors the attitudes of the Pharisees and Sadducees, who discredited Jesus and the Kingdom of Heaven because it did not fit into their limited understanding. As Jesus warned, such attitudes make it harder for people to enter into the Kingdom of Heaven.

It is my hope and prayer that those who struggle with these beliefs may find healing and freedom, so they can offer the compassionate, comprehensive care that all survivors deserve. There is a prayer resource for people struggling with a legalistic mindset and/or religious spirit in the resources section at the conclusion of this book.

STATEMENTS SRA SURVIVORS MAY SAY

The following statements are examples of things survivors of SRA trafficking may express. They are provided for awareness and educational purposes only, not for diagnosis. These insights can help service providers, counselors, ministers, and advocates recognize signs of Satanic Ritual Abuse and respond with compassion.

When a survivor shares something that may sound unusual, supernatural, or beyond your personal experience, it is essential to listen without judgment or disbelief. Their reality has been shaped by extreme trauma, manipulation, and programming. Even if what they share challenges your worldview, their experiences are real to them, and their healing depends on being heard, seen, and believed.

1.　I vividly remember being subjected to disturbing rituals that involved satanic symbols, chanting, and ceremonies.

2. I was involved with a cult-like group that practiced rituals based on satanic beliefs.
3. Members of a cult abused me physically, psychologically, and spiritually.
4. I was forced to participate in violent and harmful acts as part of satanic rituals.
5. I witnessed others being subjected to rituals, sexual abuse, and violence.
6. I often felt numb, dissociated, or experienced altered states of consciousness during or after the ritual events.
7. I believe that I was manipulated or programmed to forget or repress memories related to the abuse.
8. My trafficking happened at ritual locations.
9. Witchcraft was done to me by my abusers and traffickers.
10. My abusers would often put burns or marks on my body in patterns.
11. I was pulled out of my body and abused in the spirit realm.
12. I have suffered with being rapped by demons.
13. My abusers travel in the spirit realm to me at night.
14. I was forced to endure programming and conditioning. I had to obey, or I was tortured.
15. My father and mother were the first people who sexually abused and sold me.
16. I was forced to endure several types of torture and interrogation.
17. There were occult groups, councils, lodges, or covens involved in controlling me.

18. I was forced to give permission, sign contracts, or be in covenant with people, demons, and places.
19. I was forced out of my body to travel to altars and programming locations at night.
20. The Kabbalah was involved in my abuse.
21. I think I have a device or microchip that they put in me.
22. My traffickers used scriptures and twisted them during rituals, ceremonies, and abuse.
23. My traffickers told me that Satan is god and I was forced to worship him.
24. Some parts of me were given jobs and titles/names by my abusers.
25. My abusers speak in code words to me and text me pictures of symbols, which is very triggering and confusing.

TOUCH, DEVICES, AND ENVIRONMENTAL TRIGGERS

Survivors may have trauma around specific colors, words, music, symbols, and even touch. For example, certain gestures (like shoulder taps) may be associated with rituals. It is important for service providers to be aware of the potential triggers that could re-traumatize these individuals, including how they touch or hug them.

Victims of trafficking and SRA have experienced physical and sexual abuse at the hands of their abusers. This can result in a heightened sensitivity to touch and physical contact, and it may be triggering for them to be touched without their consent. Even seemingly innocent gestures, like patting someone on the shoulder, can bring back memories of past abuse and cause emotional distress.

It is crucial for service providers to be sensitive to the victim's body language and personal space, and to ask for their permission before touching or hugging them. This is true trauma-informed care that protects felt safety, while honoring and empowering survivor choice. Victims of trafficking and SRA need to feel that they have control over their own bodies and personal space, and that their boundaries are being respected. Asking for permission before touching can also help to establish trust and build a rapport with the victim.

Service providers should not take it personally if a victim says no to physical contact. This is not a reflection of their own actions, but rather a reflection of the victim's trauma and their need for control over their own body. Instead, service providers should continue to offer support and care for the victim in other ways, while respecting their boundaries and choices.

Using the same example: repeatedly patting an SRA survivor on the shoulder, to "encourage" them, may be triggering because it is how a ritual is started and coded with that victim. Remember the Kabbalah Tree points.

DEVICES

In recent years, technological advancements have introduced devices like Neuralink's brain-computer interfaces, which implant microchips into the brain to facilitate direct communication with computers. While these innovations aim to enhance human capabilities, similar technologies are misused for malicious purposes. Devices have been used within SRA, Trafficking, and government mind-controlled victims for many years.

Inner Ear Devices - Some victims may undergo surgeries to implant devices in the inner ear, enabling traffickers to access the vagal nerve through methods like Morse code tapping or direct speech. This can result in victims displaying behaviors such as finger-tapping patterns during dissociative episodes and switching personality parts.

Subdermal Tracking Implants - Traffickers may implant tracking devices beneath the victim's skin, similar to pet microchips, to monitor their location and prevent escape. These implants facilitate continuous exploitation by allowing abusers to locate and control victims at all times.

REMOVING OCCULT ITEMS AND MARKINGS

SRA victims are often subjected to physical, emotional, and psychological trauma, and the cult's use of cursed jewelry, tattoos, and other ritual items can add to their distress. These items can be powerful reminders of their traumatic experiences and their connection to programming, curses, and the cult.

Removing these items can be a significant step toward healing and finding freedom from the cult's influence. When the survivor is ready, it is important to support them in this process. It must be their choice to get rid of these items, as they may have conflicting emotions about them. It is essential to provide them with a safe and non-judgmental environment to express their feelings and make their own decisions.

The process of removing these items can be liberating for many reasons. It represents the survivor overcoming their fear of the cult members and breaking any agreements or contracts connected with the gifts of jewelry or tattoos. It is also a physical act of taking back control over their body and their life. Removing these items can be a symbolic representation of the survivor's journey toward healing and reclaiming their power.

It is crucial to ensure that the survivor has access to professional support during this process. They may need emotional support, counseling, or medical attention, depending on their individual needs. It is important to work with trained professionals who have experience working with survivors of complex trauma and ritual abuse.

INVESTIGATION TIP FOR LAW ENFORCEMENT

For Law Enforcement, when doing investigations, know that often the Cult Leaders and Satanists usually have a locked file cabinet with copies of "contracts" that they forced victims to sign during torture and abuse, a forced "agreement." This is how they convince the victims that they have "legal rights" to do whatever they want to them, and that the victim will be criminalized if they ever tell. For the sake of investigations, if found, it would reveal victim's names and crimes against them. These contracts may also reveal lodges or businesses involved in the crimes against the victims.

COMMISSIONING: THE MANTLE AND ANOINTING OF REFORMERS

You were born for such a time as this. Just as King Josiah tore down the altars of Molech and defiled the places where children were ritually abused and sacrificed in fire... just as King Asa banished shrine prostitution (trafficking) and destroyed generational idols... and just as the prophet Elijah called down the fire of God from heaven and confronted the false occult prophets of Baal and Asherah on Mount Carmel—so too are you called to rise up in this generation with holy boldness and unwavering faith.

The same Holy Spirit that raised Jesus from the dead lives inside of you. We are not powerless. We will not bow to fear. We are carriers of Kingdom authority. The blood of Jesus is stronger than any ritual, spell, incantation, or curse. The name of Jesus is higher than every occult power. And the victory of Jesus is final over every satanic agenda.

It is time to take your stand. Do not be intimidated by witches, Satanists, or traffickers. They operate from a place of deception and defeat. You, however, stand in resurrection power. You are called to confront darkness, not coexist with it. Step forward in the authority of Christ and carry the anointing and mantle of Josiah, Asa, and Elijah—tearing down strongholds, confronting evil, eradicating ritual trafficking, and restoring what rightfully belongs to the Kingdom of God.

The battle is real, but so is the victory. Heaven is backing you. And the Lord is commissioning you now to rise as a righteous reformer in this generation—for His glory, by His power, and in His name.

1 Kings 18:21-40 NASB (Elijah Calls Down Fire on Mount Carmel)

Elijah came near to all the people and said, "How long *will* you hesitate between two opinions? If the Lord is God, follow Him; but if Baal, follow him." But the people did not answer him a word. Then Elijah said to the people, "I alone am left a prophet of the Lord, but Baal's prophets are 450 men. Now let them give us two oxen; and let them choose one ox for themselves and cut it up, and place it on the wood, but put no fire *under it;* and I will prepare the other ox and lay it on the wood, and I will not put a fire *under it.* Then you call on the name of your god, and I will call on the name of the Lord, and the God who answers by fire, He is God." And all the people said, "That is a good idea."

So Elijah said to the prophets of Baal, "Choose one ox for yourselves and prepare it first for you are many, and call on the name of your god, but put no fire *under it.*" Then they took the ox which was given them and they prepared it and called on the name of Baal from morning until noon saying, "O Baal, answer us." But there was no voice and no one answered. And they leaped about the altar which they made. It came about at noon that Elijah mocked them and said, "Call out with a loud voice, for he is a god; either he is occupied or gone aside, or is on a journey, or perhaps he is asleep and needs to be awakened." So, they cried with a loud voice and cut themselves according to their custom with swords and lances until the blood gushed out on them. When midday was past, they raved until the time of the offering of the *evening* sacrifice; but there was no voice, no one answered, and no one paid attention.

Then Elijah said to all the people, "Come near to me." So, all the people came near to him. And he repaired the altar of the Lord, which had been torn down. Elijah took twelve stones according to the number of the tribes of the sons of Jacob, to whom the word of the Lord had come, saying, "Israel shall be your name." So. with the stones he built an altar in the name of the Lord, and he made a trench around the altar, large enough to hold two measures of seed. Then he arranged the wood and cut the ox in pieces, and laid *it* on the wood. And he said, "Fill four pitchers with water and pour *it* on the burnt offering and the wood." And he said, "Do it a second time," and they did it a second time. And he said, "Do it a third time," and they did it a third time. The water flowed around the altar, and he also filled the trench with water.

Elijah's Prayer

At the time of the offering of the *evening* sacrifice, Elijah the prophet came near and said, "O Lord, the God of Abraham, Isaac, and Israel, today let it be known that You are God in Israel and that I am Your servant and I have done all these things at Your word. Answer me, O Lord, answer me, that this people may know that You, O Lord, are God, and *that* You have turned their heart back again." Then the fire of the Lord fell and consumed the burnt offering and the wood and the stones and the dust, and licked up the water that was in the trench. When all the people saw it, they fell on their faces; and they said, "The Lord, He is God; the Lord, He is God." Then Elijah said to them, "Seize the prophets of Baal; do not let one of them escape." So they seized them; and Elijah brought them down to the brook Kishon, and slew them there.

2 Kings 23:10, 24-25 NLT (King Josiah destroys all Pagan Temples and Idol Worship.)

"Then the king defiled the altar of Topheth in the valley of Ben-Hinnom, so no one could ever again use it to sacrifice a son or daughter in the fire as an offering to Molech... (24-25) Josiah also got rid of the mediums and psychics, the household gods, the idols, and every other kind of detestable practice, both in Jerusalem and throughout the land of Judah. He did this in obedience to the laws written in the scroll that Hilkiah the priest had found in the Lord's

Temple. Never before had there been a king like Josiah, who turned to the Lord with all his heart and soul and strength, obeying all the laws of Moses. And there has never been a king like him since."

1 Kings 15:12-15 NLT (King Asa Banishes Shrine Prostitutes)

"Asa did what was pleasing in the Lord's sight, as his ancestor David had done. He banished the male and female shrine prostitutes from the land and got rid of all the idols his ancestors had made. He even deposed his grandmother, Maacah, from her position as queen mother because she had made an obscene Asherah pole. He cut down her obscene pole and burned it in the Kidron Valley. Although the pagan shrines were not removed, Asa's heart remained completely faithful to the Lord throughout his life. He brought into the Temple of the Lord the silver and gold and the various items that he and his father had dedicated."

ADDITIONAL RESOURCES

Out of Shadows documentary: www.intothelight.movie

Resource library: www.SulaLael.com → "Training Resource Library" in the Website Footer → Password: ITMresources

PERSONAL PRAYER PROMPTS

1. I repent for and renounce all witchcraft and occult involvement.
   In the name of Jesus, I repent for every way I or my ancestors have knowingly or unknowingly participated in witchcraft, manipulation, New Age practices, false religions, or any occult activity. I place the blood of Jesus over these open doors and declare them closed and locked now.

2. I renounce fear and every spirit of intimidation. I break the agreement with fear, terror, and every lie that says I am powerless. I declare that the perfect love of God casts out fear, and I choose to stand in the authority Jesus has given me.

3. I renounce every lie that witchcraft or Satan is more powerful than Jesus.
   I reject the lie that curses, rituals, or demonic forces have greater power than the name of Jesus. I declare that the blood of Jesus is stronger than any spell, ritual, or programming and His victory is final.

4. In the name of Jesus, I command every unclean spirit to leave.
   I speak to every demon and stronghold connected to what I have renounced, and I command you to leave me and my household now in Jesus' name. You have no more legal right. I am covered by the blood of Jesus and sealed by the Holy Spirit.

5. I receive the mantle and anointing of Elijah, Josiah, and Asa.
   Lord, I receive Your commissioning to rise as a righteous reformer in my generation. Anoint me with boldness, purity, and holy authority to stand for truth, justice, and freedom.

6. I declare Jesus is Lord over every system of darkness.
   I declare that no matter how hidden or complex Satanic Ritual Abuse networks may be, Jesus has already overcome in every realm. His blood speaks a better word. His authority dismantles every system of abuse.

7. Jesus, what do You want to say to me, show me, or reveal to me?
   I pause now and open my heart to Your voice. Speak truth into the places that fear once lived. Reveal what You want me to understand about the spiritual war and the authority You've given me to walk in victory.

NOTES

CHAPTER 8

WHAT SATANISTS AND OCCULT TRAFFICKERS
DON'T WANT YOU TO KNOW

#1 SHAME IS THE FOUNDATION OF SATAN'S
GOVERNMENT

"At that moment their eyes were opened, and they suddenly felt shame at their nakedness. So they sewed fig leaves together to cover themselves." (Genesis 3:7 NLT)

Shame has been a powerful tool used by Satan since the beginning of humanity, as seen in the story of Adam and Eve's disobedience in the Garden of Eden. When they ate fruit from the tree of the knowledge of good and evil, they experienced shame for the first time, a feeling that Satan exploited to further separate them from God.

Individuals who have suffered the unimaginable pain of satanic ritual abuse and sex trafficking are often plagued by an overwhelming sense of shame. The Shame demon is deliberately placed in victims by their abusers first to control and manipulate them, making it easier to maintain power over their victims. Shame can act as a stronghold, enabling further trauma and fragmentation of the individual.

As followers of Christ, our mission is to help these individuals find freedom from the burden of shame and the darkness that surrounds them. Through the transformative power of Jesus Christ, we can support their journey toward healing and wholeness. Deliverance and deprogramming are essential components of this process, as they enable survivors to break free from the chains of shame that have held them captive for so long.

In our work with survivors of satanic ritual abuse and sex trafficking, we have found that addressing shame is a crucial step toward lasting freedom. If the stronghold of shame is not dismantled, it can continue to leave the door open for further harm, re-entry of demons that were just evicted, and hinder the survivor's progress. If the Shame demon and shame programming are not removed, demons will regain access to the targeted individuals. By helping them confront and overcome shame, we can close that door and help them build a stronger foundation for their healing journey.

Through faith in Jesus Christ, survivors of satanic ritual abuse and sex trafficking can experience freedom from shame and the other strongholds that have kept them bound. As they encounter God's truth, love, and forgiveness, they will begin to see themselves as worthy, valuable, and loved, allowing them to reclaim their lives and step into the fullness of their God-given purpose.

Matthew 12 43:45 Jesus Speaking... "When an evil spirit leaves a person, it goes into the desert, seeking rest but finding none. Then it says, 'I will return to the person I came from.' So it returns and finds its former home empty, swept, and in order. Then the spirit finds seven other spirits more evil than itself, and they all enter the person and live there. And so that person is worse off than before. That will be the experience of this evil generation."

WHAT DID JESUS DO TO ADDRESS SHAME?

"We do this by keeping our eyes on Jesus, the champion who initiates and perfects our faith. Because of the joy awaiting him, he endured the cross, disregarding its shame. Now he is seated in the place of honor beside God's throne." (Hebrews 12:2 NLT)

"He canceled the record of the charges against us and took it away by nailing it to the cross. In this way, he disarmed the spiritual rulers and authorities. He shamed them publicly by his victory over them on the cross." (Colossians 2:14-15 NLT)

Just as shame entered the world through a tree in the Garden of Eden, it was also on a tree—the cross—that Jesus overcame shame. He not only endured shame on our behalf, but He also publicly humiliated the enemy, shaming him, rendering their power and accusations against us null and void. This victory over shame was achieved by Jesus' willingness to suffer on the cross, and it is through His triumph that we, too, can live free from shame and condemnation.

#2 RIGHTEOUSNESS

So, if shame is the foundation of Satan's government, what is the foundation of God's government?

"Righteousness and justice are the foundation of your throne."— *Psalm 89:14, ESV*

"For the kingdom of God is not a matter of rules about food and drink, but is in the realm of the Holy Spirit, filled with righteousness, peace, and joy." — *Romans 14:17, TPT*

"So above all, constantly chase after the realm of God's kingdom and the righteousness that proceeds from him. Then all these less important things will be given to you abundantly."— *Matthew 6:33, TPT*

These three scriptures give us a profound understanding of what it means to live under the rule and reign of God. His Kingdom is built on righteousness—a spiritual reality that protects, empowers, and transforms.

Psalm 89:14 tells us that "righteousness and justice are the foundation of [God's] throne." This means God governs from a place of perfect purity, moral excellence, and justice. Righteousness is not merely a concept; it is the very atmosphere of His rule, ensuring fairness and divine order.

Romans 14:17 echoes this truth, emphasizing that the Kingdom of God is not about religious rules or outward rituals, but about the inner transformation brought by the Holy Spirit—where righteousness, peace, and joy become the markers of our lives. This righteousness is not earned; it is imparted to us by faith through Christ, changing the way we think, live, and relate to others.

And then, Matthew 6:33 reminds us to seek first His Kingdom and His righteousness. Why? Because this is the place of divine protection and power. When we are anchored in righteousness, we are no longer vulnerable to the tactics of the enemy. Purity repels darkness. When we allow God to sanctify every area of our lives, we close the doors that Satan often exploits.

Jesus Himself said, *"I won't speak with you much longer, for the ruler of this dark world is coming. But he has no power over me, for he has nothing to use against me." —John 14:30, TPT.*

When we walk in the righteousness of Christ, the enemy cannot find a foothold in us. His weapons may form, but they will not prosper (Isaiah 54:17). Our obedience and alignment with God's Kingdom make us dangerous to darkness.

This is not just a theological truth—it is a spiritual strategy for overcoming warfare, temptation, and cycles of shame. God's righteousness is both our foundation and our defense.

For a deeper dive into this revelation and how righteousness impacts your identity and freedom from shame, be sure to read my book *The Unashamed Bride*.

Through the finished work of the cross, we can obtain the gift of God's righteousness. The blood of Jesus Christ, our Savior, was shed to cleanse us of our sins and empower us to live a life aligned with God's government and Kingdom realm (Hebrews 9:14, Ephesians 1:7). Scripture tells us that Jesus became sin for us so that we could become the righteousness of God in Him (2 Corinthians 5:21).

Additionally, we are not left to navigate this life alone; we have the help and guidance of the Holy Spirit. As Jesus promised, the Holy Spirit is our Comforter and Advocate, who will teach us all things and guide us in truth (John 14:16-17, 26). By relying on the Holy Spirit, we can experience transformation and healing.

For survivors of SRA trafficking, this message is particularly life-changing. The power of Christ's sacrifice and the Holy Spirit's presence can cleanse and restore their sense of worth, lifting them out of

Shame, the foundation of Satan's government, that has weighed them down. They can experience a renewed life, clean and pure, as they embrace the righteousness available through Jesus and God's Kingdom.

It is possible to overcome the shame and darkness that Satan seeks to impose and to live in the higher reality of God's love and grace (1 John 1:9, Romans 8:1). By placing their faith in Jesus Christ, trafficking survivors can experience the freedom and healing that comes from the knowledge that they are no longer defined by their past, but by the righteousness of God (Isaiah 61:10).

#3 ASTRAL PROJECTION

Out of Body spiritual encounters with God are prevalent throughout the Bible, with numerous examples in the Book of Revelation, Ezekiel, Song of Songs, Isaiah, Psalms, and more. These profound experiences draw God's people closer to Him. These encounters are meant to be led by Jesus Christ and validated by the Word of God. These rapturous encounters led by Jesus never contradict the Word. Jesus is the Word (John 1:1-5).

In 1 Corinthians 12:1-4 TPT, Paul shares the account of someone in union with Christ who experienced an extraordinary spiritual encounter, being taken into the third heaven and hearing unspeakable secrets.

The kingdom of darkness often imitates and perverts holy experiences. Engaging in spiritual travel or activities outside of a relationship with Jesus and without adherence to His word is considered occult witchcraft. Satanists and occult members practice astral projection, where they leave their bodies to interact with the spirit realm. New Age Spiritualism portrays this as an empowering journey, but the dangers and consequences are often concealed. Those who astral project face significant spiritual warfare, engaging with demons and false angels.

Astral projection is an occult term used to describe an intentional out-of-body experience (OBE) that involves the separation of the "astral body" or "subtle body" from the physical body, allowing the individual to consciously explore the astral plane or other dimensions. This phenomenon is often associated with spiritual and paranormal experiences, as well as practices like occult meditation and lucid dreaming. Source: Encyclopedia Britannica (https://www.britannica.com/topic/astral-projection)

FORCED ASTRAL PROJECTION

Satanists, occult members, and witches can forcibly remove vulnerable victims from their bodies through what I refer to as "forced astral projection," subjecting them to programming, rituals, demonic rape, astral assaults, curses, and torment. Most SRA (Satanic Ritual Abuse) trafficking survivors have experienced this. When it occurs, it is often the result of coerced agreements—such as covenants, promises, permissions, or contracts—made under the extreme duress of rituals, trauma, torture, or programming. If there is generational iniquity, those agreements have already been made. However, this also represents the highest level of spiritual warfare, even in cases where no legal right or access was knowingly granted to Satan. There are also individuals with no history of SRA who have encountered similar forms of warfare.

Let's take a look at how Jesus dealt with the highest level of warfare in the spiritual realm.

Jesus, aware of forced astral projection as a form of Satan-led warfare, demonstrated how to overcome it in the following scripture. He humbled himself to endure persecution and warfare, being pulled from his body by Satan to a location. He was Holy, perfect, and without sin, yet experienced the highest level of warfare that exists in order to show us a strategy for victory. Jesus understands. He showed us how to break free from this type of attack with the Word of God.

"And the third time the accuser lifted Jesus up onto a very high mountain range and showed him all the kingdoms of the world and all the splendor that goes with it. All of these kingdoms I will give to you," the accuser said, "if only you will kneel down before me and worship me. But Jesus said, "Go away, Satan! For the Scriptures say: Kneel before the Lord your God and worship only him." At once, the accuser left him, and angels suddenly gathered around Jesus to minister to his needs." (Matthew 4:8-11 TPT)

"That is why the Scriptures say, 'When he ascended to the heights, he led a crowd of captives and gave gifts to his people. Notice that it says "he ascended." This clearly means that Christ also descended to our lowly world. And the same one who descended is the one who ascended higher than all the heavens, so that he might fill the entire universe with himself. Now these are the gifts Christ gave to the church: the apostles, the prophets, the evangelists, and the pastors and teachers." (Ephesians 4:8-11)

Jesus literally went into every place in the spirit realm, set captives free and conquered astral projection torture and captivity for all of us!

THE POWER OF GOD DURING ASTRAL ATTACKS

When Satanists, witches, and occult members engage in astral projection, they become spiritually vulnerable—something they desperately try to keep hidden. A silver cord connects their spirit to their physical body, and the farther they travel from it, the more susceptible they become to harm. Despite this risk, they depend on the ignorance and fear of many Christians to operate freely.

They often astral project to victims in order to reinforce programming, torment them, rape them, and keep them trapped in fear and control. In addition, Satanists and occult members may attempt to astral project to individuals who are helping SRA survivors, hoping to curse, intimidate, or discourage them from continuing their support.

But we do not need to fear them.

You may have heard someone say something like, "A black figure showed up in the room at night. It was a person, not a demon." This is often the result of astral projection.

To confront these attacks, believers must respond with authority and without fear. We must immediately invite the presence of Jesus and declare the Word of God. Dissociating or passively hoping the attack will end does not work—fear and inaction only empower the enemy. I strongly urge you to preach the gospel to the astral projecting individual and ask them to convert their life to Jesus. This usually causes them to leave immediately because of the explosive power of the death, burial, and resurrection of Jesus Christ. Release God's love over them. I believe that one day in heaven, I will meet people who walked away from the occult and chose Jesus—because of the prayers I prayed for them and the unwavering stand I took to present the power of the Gospel, even when they tried to attack me.

Ecclesiastes 12:6 references the *silver cord of life*, emphasizing the urgency of remembering God before the cord is broken. This cord is what connects the spirit and body during astral travel. The good news is—we have the upper hand in Christ!

Those who astral project to torment, curse, program, or abuse do not want you to know that we can cut their silver cord using the sword of the Spirit, which is the Word of God. They fear this deeply because once the cord is severed, it can become nearly impossible for them to return to their bodies. If a witch, occultist, or Satanist realizes you carry this knowledge and authority, they won't target you again—the risk is simply too high.

However, this authority must be used with reverence and obedience.

1. NEVER cut a silver cord without first preaching the Gospel to the astral projected individual. Plead with them to receive Jesus as their Lord and Savior. God's desire is that none should perish, but that all should come to repentance (2 Peter 3:9).

2. NEVER cut a cord without direct instruction from the Lord. We do not have the right to make these decisions/judgments on our own. Acting outside of God's command is disobedience and sin. We must be led by His Spirit in all things.

In Scripture, we see an example of this in the book of Ezekiel. God brought the prophet into the spirit realm and instructed him to cut a cord using the spiritual sword. As Ezekiel prophesied in faith and obedience to God's Word, it resulted in the death of a territorial occult leader. This was not human judgment—it was the execution of God's righteous judgment.

"Evil Rulers to Be Judged

Moreover, the Spirit lifted me up and brought me to the east gate of the Lord's house, which faced eastward. And behold, *there were* twenty-five men at the entrance of the gate, and among them I saw

Jaazaniah, son of Azzur, and Pelatiah, son of Benaiah, leaders of the people. He said to me, "Son of man, these are the men who devise iniquity and give evil advice in this city, who say, '*The time* is not near to build houses. This *city* is the pot and we are the flesh.' Therefore, prophesy against them, son of man, prophesy!"

> Then the Spirit of the Lord fell upon me, and He said to me, "Say, 'Thus says the Lord, "So you think, house of Israel, for I know your thoughts. You have multiplied your slain in this city, filling its streets with them." Therefore, thus says the Lord God, "Your slain whom you have laid in the midst of the city are the flesh, and this *city* is the pot; but I will bring you out of it. You have feared a sword; so I will bring a sword upon you," the Lord God declares. "And I will bring you out of the midst of the city and deliver you into the hands of strangers and execute judgments against you. You will fall by the sword. I will judge you to the border of Israel; so you shall know that I am the Lord. This *city* will not be a pot for you, nor will you be flesh in the midst of it, *but* I will judge you to the border of Israel. Thus, you will know that I am the Lord; for you have not walked in My statutes nor have you executed My ordinances, but have acted according to the ordinances of the nations around you." Now it came about as I prophesied, that Pelatiah, son of Benaiah died."-Ezekiel 11:1-13 (NASB)

Ultimately, it must be Jesus who instructs you to cut their cord. But feel free to tell them that if they don't stop traveling in the spirit to you, their cord will be cut. They will leave fast and not come back.

The fear of the Lord is the beginning of wisdom (Proverbs 9:10). We as believers must not underestimate this power and authority that we have been given. Praying for the salvation of occult members and sharing the gospel with them can lead to their departure from dark practices. What does Jesus instruct us to do when people curse us?

Matthew 5:44 calls believers to love their enemies, bless those who curse them, and pray for those who persecute them. By following Jesus' teachings and applying the spiritual gifts provided by Him, Christians can counteract the strategies of Satanists and occult members, protecting victims and spreading the light of Christ.

#4 SATANIST AND OCCULT STRATEGIES AFTER A VICTIM ESCAPES

The following is a list of things to actively keep in prayer regarding the SRA survivors that you are ministering to or assisting. These are the first things that Satanists and Witches do in order to attempt to regain control and force the victim to return to them.

1. Deploying demons: Traffickers may attempt to send demons associated with their specific programming and roles within the cult (e.g., Baphomet, Lilith, suicide, beast, python, icubus

and succubus, affliction, infirmity, insanity, sexual perversion/lust, false gods and goddesses, etc.). These demons can make it difficult for survivors to break free from their abusers' control.

2. Astral projection: Traffickers may use astral projection to communicate, intimidate, and reinforce programming. They may also utilize forced astral projection to forcibly pull survivors from their bodies and subject them to further programming, rapes, abuse, and torture. They give false promises that the torture will stop if they return to the cult.

3. Exploiting trauma and nightmares: Occult members look for unhealed trauma within survivors. They seek to access unhealed/unintegrated trapped parts/alters and focus on the trauma of those parts. They work with Satan to send nightmares or trigger dissociative states to manipulate and regain control over them.

4. Rituals and curses: Traffickers may gather to perform rituals and cast curses against survivors and those attempting to help them, in hopes of maintaining control and instilling fear. The most common window of time used is 12 am-3 am. They are very persistent and believe that they can wear out the individual and the Christians helping. However, we have more power through Christ.

We must be solid in our faith. **Prayers are more powerful than curses!** You have to move in the unwavering truth that curses can't land on you when you are hidden in Christ and a relationship with Him.

"Like a fluttering sparrow or a darting swallow, an undeserved curse will not land on its intended victim." -Proverbs 26:2

#5 THE POWER AND AUTHORITY WE HAVE THROUGH JESUS

- Overcoming Legalism and Religious Mindsets: It is crucial for Christians to recognize that legalism, religious spirits, and Pharisee-like mentalities hold no power against the occult. Our strength comes from a genuine relationship with God and the power of His Spirit, not from religious rituals or self-righteous attitudes. There is a prayer in the resources at the end of this book for freedom from this.
- The Power of God's Word: As believers, we have been equipped with the mighty Word of God to wage spiritual warfare against the forces of darkness. The Bible's teachings, as well as the dreams and visions God has imparted to us, are not just symbolic but carry real, authoritative power. By accessing these divine gifts through faith, we can stand firm against any spiritual attack.
- Embracing Childlike Faith and Kingdom Living: Matthew 18:3 reminds us of the importance of having a childlike faith. Jesus called a child to His side and taught His disciples that humility

and teachability were essential qualities for entering the kingdom of heaven. To live from the power and authority of the Kingdom of God, while here on earth, we must have child-like faith.

- Demonstrating God's Power, Not Just Words: 1 Corinthians 4:20 emphasizes that the kingdom of God comes with power, not merely impressive words. Our actions and the way we live our lives should reflect the transformative power of God's kingdom, rather than relying on empty rhetoric. We must have faith that the Kingdom of God is more powerful than the kingdom of darkness. The Gospel is explosive power!

- Seeking God's Kingdom and Righteousness First: In Matthew 6:33, Jesus exhorts us to prioritize seeking God's kingdom and righteousness above all else. When we do so, all other necessities will be provided for us. As we pursue God's kingdom and live righteously, we can confidently face any challenge, including Satanists and occult traffickers, knowing that God's power is on our side.

By embracing these principles, Christians can confidently stand against Satanists and occult traffickers, knowing that we have the power and authority of the living God within us. We need not fear these adversaries, for we are more than conquerors through Christ who strengthens us (Romans 8:37).

#6 JUSTICE THROUGH PRAYER & RADICAL OBEDIENCE

As believers, we are called not only to pray but to act in radical obedience to God's will to bring healing and freedom to those enslaved by these evil practices. Scripture is clear about the power of prayer, and it is our weapon in this spiritual battle.

THE POWER OF PRAYER

The Bible is filled with powerful examples of the importance of prayer in the lives of believers. Through prayer, we can access God's divine intervention and supernatural power.

James 5:16 (TPT) states, "Confess and acknowledge how you have offended one another and then pray for one another to be instantly healed, for tremendous power is released through the passionate, heartfelt prayer of a godly believer!"

Ephesians 6:18 (TPT) instructs us to, "Pray passionately in the Spirit, as you constantly intercede with every form of prayer at all times. Pray the blessings of God upon all his believers."

As we pray for the victims of SRA and sex trafficking, we are invoking God's authority and power to break the chains of bondage and bring restoration.

There are times when we are discouraged by severely delayed or failed justice by way of the courts and judicial system on earth. However, justice can be sought through intercession in the Courtroom of Heaven. It is referenced several times throughout scripture, and Jesus even teaches this prayer through strategy. There is a teaching about the Courtroom of Heaven in the resources section at the end of this book. This is a method of bringing a massive break-through for victims of trafficking.

RADICAL OBEDIENCE

Prayer is the starting point, but it should not be the end of our involvement. Radical obedience means actively responding to the Holy Spirit's leading and stepping out of our comfort zones to be the hands and feet of Jesus. Obeying the Lord is how the war is won. He will give you scriptures to declare that have explosive power against the enemy and the oc-cult traffickers targeting the survivors you're working with.

In Isaiah 1:17 (TPT), we are commanded to, "Learn what it means to do what is good by seeking righteousness and justice! Rescue the oppressed. Uphold the rights of the fatherless and defend the widow's cause."

Matthew 25:40 (TPT) also reminds us that, "And to the extent that you did it for one of the least of these brothers and sisters of mine, you did it for me."

THE IMPACT OF RADICAL OBEDIENCE

In the battle against evil, radical obedience to God releases explosive Kingdom power. When individuals respond with wholehearted surrender and fierce devotion, spiritual atmospheres shift, hidden wickedness is exposed, and strongholds of oppression begin to crumble. We've already seen this truth reflected in the lives of King Josiah, King Asa, and the prophet Elijah—leaders who boldly confronted darkness in their day. Their unwavering obedience disrupted demonic systems, tore down altars of evil, and catalyzed national repentance. This is what radical obedience looks like in action: refusing to bow to fear, refusing to compromise with evil, and carrying out God's will no matter the cost.

STEP INTO RADICAL OBEDIENCE

If God could use kings under the Old Covenant to destroy Satanic systems, how much more can He use those of us under the New Covenant, filled with His Spirit and anointed for battle?

"The people who know their God shall be strong, and carry out great exploits."— *Daniel 11:32 NKJV*

"For the weapons of our warfare are not carnal but mighty through God for pulling down strongholds."— *2 Corinthians 10:4 NKJV*

God is raising a new generation of Elijahs, Josiahs and Asas—leaders, intercessors, advocates, ministers, and survivors—who demonstrate the Kingdom of God while walking in righteousness, spiritual authority, and radical obedience. You don't need a title or a throne. You need a yielded heart and a fierce yes to God.

When you step into that anointing, you will tear down altars, demolish rituals, help victims escape, and drive darkness out of territories.

THE VICTORY BELONGS TO GOD

As we engage in this spiritual battle, it is crucial to remember that the ultimate victory belongs to God. While we may face setbacks, opposition, and discouragement, we must hold onto the truth that God is in control and that He will bring justice in His perfect timing.

Romans 12:19 (TPT) assures us, "Beloved, don't be obsessed with taking revenge, but leave that to God's righteous justice. For the Scriptures say:

'Vengeance is mine, and I will repay,' says the Lord."

As Christians, we must take up the mandate of prayer and radical obedience to address the evil of satanic ritual abuse and sex trafficking. By doing so, we can partner with God in the work of redemption, healing, and justice for the oppressed. Let us be emboldened by the Holy Spirit to fight against this darkness and bring the love, hope, and light of Christ to those who desperately need it.

#7 WARFARE THROUGH INTIMACY WITH JESUS

"Now you are ready, my bride, to come with me as we climb the highest peaks together. Come with me through the archway of trust. We will look down from the crest of the glistening mounts and from the summit of our sublime sanctuary. Together, we will wage war in the lion's den and the leopard's lair as they watch nightly for their prey. For you reach into my heart. With one flash of your eyes, I am undone by your love, my beloved, my equal, my bride. You leave me breathless—I am overcome by merely a glance from your worshiping eyes, for you have stolen my heart. I am held hostage by your love and by the graces of righteousness shining upon you. How satisfying to me, my equal, my bride. Your love is my finest wine—intoxicating and thrilling. And your sweet, perfumed praises—so exotic, so pleasing." (Song of Songs 4:8-10 TPT)

The scripture from Song of Songs 4:8-10 TPT provides us with a powerful message of love, intimacy, and strength in our relationship with Jesus as our bridegroom. There are several prayer and warfare strategies that we find throughout scripture. Let's explore the strategy of spiritual warfare through intimacy with Jesus, as we work to bring freedom to victims of sex trafficking.

1. The Power of Intimacy with Jesus, Our Bridegroom
   As we face the atrocities of satanic ritual abuse and sex trafficking, it's crucial to recognize that our most potent weapon is our intimate relationship with Jesus, our bridegroom. Through this relationship, we can access His power and authority, which enables us to wage war against the powers of darkness that perpetuate these acts. We must prioritize our intimacy with Jesus, allowing His love to fill and empower us as we engage in this spiritual battle.

2. The Archway of Trust
   Intimacy with Jesus requires trust in His love, guidance, and protection. As we walk through the archway of trust with Jesus, we are equipped for spiritual warfare. This trust is developed as we spend time in prayer, meditation on His Word, and submission to His will. As we deepen our trust in Jesus, we become more confident in facing the challenges of assisting those trapped in satanic ritual abuse and sex trafficking.

3. Waging War Together
   Jesus, our bridegroom, invites us to wage war together with Him against the enemy from the place of being seated with Him in the Heavenly realm (Ephesians 2:6). As we join forces with Jesus, we can face the lion's den and leopard's lair below us on earth with courage and conviction. Jesus' presence and power in

our lives give us the strength and wisdom to stand against the forces of evil from a Heavenly perspective.

4. The Power of Praise and Worship
    Song of Songs 4:10 highlights the power of our praises and worship to Jesus. In the face of darkness, our praise and worship can be a powerful weapon against the enemy. As we exalt Jesus through praise and worship, His presence and power are released into the spiritual realm, breaking chains and setting captives free. Let us not neglect the importance of worship as a part of our spiritual warfare strategy.

5. The Intoxicating Love of Jesus
    In the midst of the battle against trafficking, it's essential to remember that Jesus' love is our source of strength, courage, and victory. His love is intoxicating and thrilling, providing us with the motivation and endurance needed to continue the fight. Not only are we undone by His love, but He is undone by ours. As we experience Jesus' love, we are enabled to love and serve others, even to love our enemies.

The strategy of spiritual warfare through intimacy with Jesus as our bridegroom is vital in our fight against satanic ritual abuse and sex trafficking. As we develop our trust in Jesus, wage war together with Him, engage in praise and worship, and experience His intoxicating love, we will be empowered and equipped to bring freedom, healing, and hope to the victims of these terrible crimes. Let us commit ourselves to this intimate love, knowing that our bridegroom, Jesus, is with us every step of the way.

PERSONAL PRAYER PROMPTS

1. Freedom from Shame
    Jesus, I bring You every layer of shame that has ever been spoken over me, placed on me, or embedded in my soul. I believe You bore my shame on the cross and triumphed over it. I receive Your cleansing love. I am no longer defined by my past. I am defined by Your righteousness and redemption.

2. Receiving the Gift of Righteousness
    Father, I receive the gift of righteousness through Christ Jesus. I choose to come under the covering of Your Kingdom, where righteousness, peace, and joy rule. Sanctify me, protect me, and purify my heart, mind, and body. Make me a living demonstration of Your holiness in a world drowning in compromise. Jesus, I receive your robe of righteousness now.

3. Protection Against Astral Assaults
    Jesus, I plead Your blood over my body, soul, and spirit as well as over my family and home. I ask You to block every form of astral projection, forced or voluntary, sent against me or anyone I love. Teach me how to respond with boldness, faith, love, and truth when spiritual attacks come. I choose to dwell in Your Psalm 91 shelter and walk in the authority of Your name. I will follow your instruction during warfare, Jesus.

4. Intercession for Occult Members to Know Jesus
   Lord, I pray for every person trapped in the occult, witchcraft, and Satanism. I ask You to break through their darkness with Your light. I pray for those who have projected into my space or harassed me spiritually—let them encounter Your overwhelming love and come to repentance. I bless those who have cursed me and spoken all evil over me. May Your kindness lead them to salvation.

5. Deliverance from Spiritual Contracts and Ritual Agreements
   Jesus, I repent for any agreements made knowingly or under duress in rituals, programming, or generational sin. I renounce and break every demonic contract, covenant, or curse—past or present. I declare that You are my only Lord and King. Cover every part of me in Your living water and the power of Your blood. Jesus, bring deliverance to every place of captivity. I ask for complete freedom, Jesus.

6. Radical Obedience and Kingdom Boldness
   Holy Spirit, give me the grace to obey You without hesitation. Teach me how to hear Your voice, follow Your strategies, and walk in Your power that destroys the works of the devil.

7. Jesus, what do you want to say to me, show me, or reveal to me? (Wait on the Lord in His presence. Journal what you see, hear, or feel He is revealing to you.)

NOTES

CHAPTER 9

SRA TRAFFICKING SURVIVOR AFTERCARE OPTIONS

AFTER IDENTIFICATION AND BEFORE ESTABLISHING A CARE PLAN

Build Trust with SRA Survivors before jumping straight into counseling, therapy, prayer, or deliverance sessions. It's crucial to acknowledge the profound trauma SRA survivors have experienced, often at the hands of individuals claiming to be "therapists" or manipulators wielding mind control. Gaining their trust can sometimes be a challenge. Before delving into deep sessions with new people, consider holding a casual "get-to-know-you" meeting. This allows the survivor to establish rapport and become more at ease with the individual intent on aiding their healing journey. Notably, when SRA survivors are triggered, a prevalent trauma response is the "fawn/friend" reaction, leading them to comply and pretend to be ok, even if it harms them internally. There's a risk of an SRA survivor acquiescing to a counseling or prayer session just to appease or get through it and get it over with. Familiarity with the person guiding the session can foster trust, paving the way for genuine healing.

SETTING THE PACE FOR HEALING

Empowering the survivor to determine the speed of their healing journey is pivotal. Pushing them to confront their profound trauma before they're mentally, emotionally, and spiritually ready could exacerbate their vulnerabilities, leading to dire consequences, such as a flight response or suicidal tendencies. Furthermore, if they're not prepared to address these deep-seated wounds, one may witness rapid "switching" where protector personalities/soul parts emerge. Equipping them with practical self-stabilization techniques before delving into intensive healing efforts is essential to the healing journey. Remember, it's often in solitude, especially at night, that the torment intensifies as they grapple with distressing trauma flashbacks/memories or confront soul and spirit trauma alone.

SELECTING THE BEST CARE OPTIONS FOR SURVIVORS

Trauma-Informed Care prioritizes SAFETY and fosters a sense of SURVIVOR CHOICE and COLLABORATION. Before implementing any care approach, it's crucial to communicate the proposed process to the survivor, allowing them to choose, and hence, prevent potential triggers. A therapeutic approach that has shown results with other survivors of sex trafficking might not necessarily be suitable for a survivor of Satanic Ritual Abuse (SRA).

For instance, consider the EMDR (Eye Movement Desensitization and Reprocessing) therapy. EMDR therapy can be a powerful tool for trauma recovery. However, it is NOT suggested for survivors of Satanic Ritual Abuse (SRA). It's imperative that practitioners adhere to ethical guidelines, which include thorough screening for dissociation before treatment. Ethical EMDR practice mandates assessing for dissociative symptoms to prevent potential harm. The International Society for the Study of Trauma and Dissociation (ISSTD) emphasizes that employing standard EMDR therapy with individuals suffering from unrecognized dissociative disorders poses significant risks. They advocate for comprehensive assessments beyond the Dissociative Experiences Scale-II (DES-II), recommending tools like the Multidimensional Inventory of Dissociation (MID) for a more accurate evaluation.

It's concerning that some EMDR practitioners, eager to apply this method with SRA survivors, bypass this critical step. Such oversight can lead to rapid switching between dissociative parts or alters and leave survivors entrenched in traumatic memories post-session. Moreover, certain EMDR techniques, including light and tapping, can inadvertently trigger memories of past rituals and programming for SRA survivors, which use the exact same approach. Therefore, it's essential to provide an unbiased, comprehensive explanation of the EMDR process to the survivor beforehand. With a thorough understanding and appropriate precautions, survivors can make informed decisions about exploring EMDR, recognizing both, its potential benefits and risks.

Similarly, this level of preparation and explanation is essential for medical appointments or spiritual engagements, like attending church services. By elucidating the process and setting expectations, survivors are reassured, enabling them to lower their trauma-induced defenses and be genuinely present. A beneficial practice includes maintaining a weekly schedule, allowing survivors to anticipate upcoming activities and seek clarifications on any concerns or uncertainties they might have.

HOLISTIC CARE OPTIONS TO CONSIDER FOR SEX TRAFFICKING SURVIVORS OF OCCULT OR SATANIC RITUAL ABUSE (SRA) - ORGANIZED BY BODY, SOUL, AND SPIRIT

BODY - Common Experiences:

1. Sexual and Physical Trauma: Survivors of occult or SRA trafficking often suffer from intentional

and severe sexual and physical trauma, leading to fragmentation and triggering trauma cycles. Some rituals may include placing sharp objects in the vagina or anus, and illegal surgeries performed on the body.

2. Occult Rituals: Survivors may have experienced curses, spells, and body markings, such as patterned burns, cuts, and bruises on specific Kabbalah points.

3. Torture: Various forms of torture, including military-style interrogation, electroshock, electric dog collars, and advanced technology for torture, have been used.

4. Dehumanization: Survivors may have endured isolation in caves, cages, closets, or confined spaces, forcing them to be still and quiet under control in traumatic conditions.

5. Devices and Injections: Survivors may have been implanted with tracking microchips, inner ear devices, or subjected to injections of various drugs and experimental substances for control and DNA manipulation.

6. Abuse of Basic Needs: Survivors may have been subjected to abusive control—withholding of food, water, and the ability to use the bathroom freely.

BODY - Care Options to Consider (when the survivor is ready):

- Medical Examination: Provide a medical examination, including a SANE rape kit and women's wellness exam (check for STDs), to address physical and sexual trauma. This also helps to identify potential evidence that can be used in court to validate the survivor's victim testimony if they choose to report their trafficking now or in the future.

- Detection and Removal of Devices: Engage medical professionals to detect and remove any implanted devices through X-rays, MRIs, and/or ultrasound wands.

- Support for Sleep and Nutrition: Offer appropriate support for sleep, such as Melatonin, and help with consistent eating and hydration.

- Support for Bathroom Use: Create a safe environment for using the bathroom, considering the possibility of past traumatic experiences in this area. The survivor may possibly need something to assist them with regular bowel movements.

SOUL - Common Experiences:

1. Fractured Soul Parts: Survivors may have fractured soul parts, each with distinct names, roles, programming, and ties to the cult, including parts programmed to lead the survivor back to the cult.

2. Programming or Conditioning: Often involving "therapist" programmers or handlers, survivors may have undergone ritualistic programming or conditioning with the goal of mind control.

3. Soul Ties: Survivors may have entered into rituals, covenants, contracts, and agreements with individuals, occult groups, and geographical locations (including elements in those locations to cause a controlled grid of entrapment).

SOUL - Care Options to Consider (when the survivor is ready):

- Trauma-Informed Counseling/Therapy: Provide counseling/therapy by experienced professionals with expertise in working with DID and SRA survivors. Integration of fractured soul parts and personalities may be facilitated by a trained professional if the survivor is seeking and desiring such integration. THIS MUST BE DONE BY AN EXPERT OR PROFESSIONAL WHEN THE SURVIVOR IS SEEKING AND DESIRING TO BE INTEGRATED. Remember, soul parts are NOT demons and cannot be cast out (which would cause more trauma and damage to the survivor if attempted).
- Survivor Mentorship: Connect survivors with others who have experienced similar journeys to instill hope and faith in their journey toward freedom and healing.
- Coping Techniques: Teach coping techniques for dealing with a dysregulated nervous system, triggers, and switching between different parts/personalities, aiming to help the survivor stay present and grounded. (See tools in the Resource Section)

- Healing the Soul: Facilitate prayers to break soul ties, covenants, contracts, permissions, and agreements, and to divorce the cult members. Additionally, prayers to renounce and divorce Satan and demons should be considered, focusing on reclaiming parts of the soul given to them. (See prayer in the Resource Section)
- De-Programming / Mind Renewal: Incorporate prayer and biblical study to deprogram (by knowing the truth that sets them free) and remove mind control, fostering the renewal of the survivor's mind in Christ. Learning lies vs truth.
- Forgiveness and Self-Acceptance: Encourage prayers for self-forgiveness and acceptance, fostering a process of allowing Jesus to interact with every part of the soul and extending love and gratitude to all the fractured parts that have kept the survivor alive. Even cult loyal parts with toxic thinking and behaviors should be forgiven and have access to the Gospel... So, they can meet Jesus and receive healing and deliverance. It is not their fault that they were tortured and programmed the way that they were.

SPIRIT / SPIRITUAL REALM - Common Experiences:

1. Survivors may have experienced forced astral projection, being taken to demonic altars, realms, or programming sites to enforce trauma, fear, trauma, and control.

2. Occult members astral projecting to the survivor, usually at night, in the spirit realm to curse, intimidate, sexually abuse, and enforce programs to maintain fear, trauma, and control.

3. Spirit Rapes: During sleep, survivors may experience spirit rapes by astral projecting occult members or demonic entities like Incubus and Succubus, aiming to traumatize and enforce control.

SPIRIT / SPIRITUAL REALM - Care Options (when the survivor is ready):

1. Non-Coercive Spiritual Engagement: Avoid immediately pressuring survivors to engage in religious activities, such as going to church or other spiritual events. Consider providing another option to them during the first phase of their time in your program so the survivor has a choice. This is also part of trauma-informed care, considering the possibility of "False Jesus Programming."

2. Water Baptism and Holy Spirit Baptism: Provide guidance and support for survivors seeking water baptism and baptism of the Holy Spirit. (Explain Well)

3. Healing the Spirit Man: Engage in prayers to heal, bless, and restore the human spirit.

4. Deliverance: Freedom from demonic spirits can be pursued, but it must be conducted lovingly and gently, respecting the survivor's readiness and avoiding triggers. This must be

done without screaming, embarrassing them in front of others, and force (which would be very triggering to the survivor). Repenting, renouncing (breaking agreement with), and forgiving strips Satan of legal rights. Then the demons must leave in the name of Jesus. Learn how to do this through the *Ministering to Sex Trafficking Survivors* Training www.takeflightsurvivors.org/academy.

*Remember, there are dissociated parts within occult and SRA survivors. Starting prayer times with something like "I repent on behalf of every part of me, in every location and on every timeline of my life..." ensures that the prayers are being done on behalf of the whole person and not just a leading presenting part. The survivor must be at a place of faith, believing the truth and knowing that they are worthy of receiving freedom, healing, and God's love.

Note: The care options listed above are intended to be implemented with great sensitivity and understanding of the survivor's unique needs and readiness. Following the leadership of Jesus and collaboration with a multidisciplinary team, including mental health professionals, Christian counselors, and trauma-informed practitioners, is crucial in providing the most comprehensive and effective care for survivors of occult or SRA trafficking.

"Now may the God of peace Himself sanctify you completely; and may your whole spirit, soul, and body be preserved blameless at the coming of our Lord Jesus Christ. He who calls you is faithful, who also will do it." -1 Thessalonians 5:23-24 NKJV

PERSONAL PRAYER PROMPTS

1. Jesus, help me build trust gently.
   Lord, I ask for Your wisdom and compassion as I walk with survivors of trafficking and SRA. Teach me how to slow down, listen with love, and create safety through consistency. Help me see beyond what is said and discern what is needed. I want to serve and minister from a place of peace and trust, following Your lead. You know what's best.

2. Give me discernment regarding survivor readiness.
   Jesus, I surrender every desire to "fix" or rush the healing process. Help me honor each survivor's pace, letting You lead every next step. Empower me to respect their no's, their pauses, their boundaries, and trust that You are working even in the waiting.

3. Jesus, guide me in selecting the right care for each survivor.
   Lord, I invite You into every decision regarding counseling, therapy, and aftercare support. Help me to discern which modalities are safe and helpful, and which may retraumatize. Remind me to discuss these options with the survivor so that they are able to collaborate in their healing care plan. Give me the courage to

speak truthfully and compassionately, and to prioritize survivor choice above all else.

4. Let my care be trauma-informed and Holy Spirit-led.

   Jesus, I ask for a deep understanding of trauma—not just through training but through the discernment of the Holy Spirit. Help me care without control, listen without assumption, and love without pressure. Lead me to respond gently, avoiding religious harm or spiritual coercion. Let my presence reflect Your kindness.

5. Jesus, help me honor survivor choice and free will.

   Lord, I acknowledge that true healing and freedom cannot be forced. You are a God who honors our free will, and I want to reflect that in every care plan, prayer session, and conversation. Help me trust that when a survivor chooses healing for themselves, it opens the door to complete healing, deliverance, deprogramming and transformation with You.

6. Jesus what do you want to say to me, show me or reveal to me? (Wait on the Lord in His presence. Journal what you see, hear or feel He is revealing to you.)

NOTES

HOW TO REPORT

POTENTIAL TRAFFICKING

Take note of Who? What? How? Where? Why? When? Any details you can remember will be helpful when making a report. What was the potential victim or trafficker wearing? What nationality? What did they look like? How old? Did they have any tattoos, scars, or marks? Vehicle model, make, color? Address?

Anytime someone is under the age of 18 and you suspect sexual abuse, physical abuse, or trafficking, you have to report it as a "Mandatory Reporter." You could go to jail if you are aware and did not report it. Anyone under the age of 18 is in the sex industry or providing sexual services to people for the benefit/gain of someone else... That minor, by legal definition, is considered a trafficking victim.

CONTACT

- Rescue America Hotline 833-599-3733
- Law Enforcement (In the county of the suspected trafficking)
- Your State Abuse Hotline
- Human Trafficking Hotline 888-373-7888

***In most cases, the victim's consent is needed in order to arrest the trafficker. A Survivor Leader Advocate is recommended to walk alongside the victim in the reporting and aftercare process.

A NOTE FROM SURVIVOR LEADER, SULA

Dear Beloved Reader,

Thank you from the depths of my heart for taking the time to journey through this book. Your willingness to engage with such weighty and complex realities is both rare and sacred. It speaks to the compassion, strength, and purpose that lives within you.

If you prayed through the prompts at the end of each chapter, thank you. Your prayers matter more than you know. They carry weight in the spirit realm... They bring God's will and Kingdom on earth as it is in Heaven. If you've been blessed by the prayer prompts, I invite you to listen to my free album, *Take Flight: Soaking Prayers and Scripture Meditation,* available wherever music is sold, including YouTube. If you love prayer, you will love this resource.

This book was not easy to write—and I know it wasn't easy to read. Yet you stayed. You leaned in. You listened. That alone sets you apart as someone who can carry this kind of truth with grace.

As you continue forward, I pray that the Lord strengthens you with wisdom, compassion, and discernment. I pray that the Holy Spirit would lead you and guide you in all truth as you take a stand against trafficking. Whether you're a survivor, a service provider, a loved one, or a concerned soul—thank you. You are part of the solution.

If you'd like to learn more or go deeper, you're warmly invited to explore the *Take Flight Academy* at

<u>www.TakeFlightSurvivors.org</u>—a place of survivor-informed learning, healing, and Kingdom equipping.

With all my gratitude and love,
Sula Lael

ADDITIONAL SUGGESTED RESOURCES

1. Duval, D. (2017). Extreme Prayers that Shake Heaven and Earth. BRIDE Ministries International.
2. Bride Ministries International. (n.d.). Coaching for SRA Survivors and D.I.D. [Web page]. Retrieved from <u>https://bridemovement.com</u>
3. Ramirez, J. (2015). Fire Prayers. Charisma House.
4. Liebscher, T. (n.d.). Shabar Ecourse & Manual. [Web page]. Retrieved from <u>https://www.teresaliebscher.com/shabar</u>
5. Ferrell, A. M. (2012). Regions of Captivity. Voice of the Light Ministries.
6. Lael, S. (2020). Fighting for Your Purpose – From Sex Trafficking to Ministry. Independently published.

SAMPLE PRAYER FOR BREAKING SOUL TIES

"Now it came about when he had finished speaking to Saul, that the soul of Jonathan was knit to the soul of David, and Jonathan loved him as himself." 1 Samuel 18:1 NASB1995

"Or do you not know that the one who joins himself to a prostitute is one body with her? For He says, "The two shall become one flesh."" 1 Corinthians 6:16 NASB1995

"and the two shall become one flesh'; so then they are no longer two, but one flesh." Mark 10:8 NKJV

Lord, I repent for all sin, transgression, and iniquities in my life... I repent for all sins that I've committed with, for or against in Jesus' name.

I repent for making   an idol in my life. Right now, I place you, God, Jesus & Holy Spirit first in my life.

I choose to forgive of all the ways has hurt me and sinned against me.

Right now, I cut and sever all soul ties and trauma bonds that I have with in Jesus' name.

I humbly ask you God to heal from any damage that I've caused. I ask that you heal me from any trauma, emotional, physical, spiritual, financial, or relational damage that they caused in me.

I bind and rebuke all demonic warfare that I've brought into life in Jesus' name. I bind and rebuke all demonic warfare that's come into my life through in Jesus' name... I command it to leave now in Jesus' name.

I give back everything that I have that belongs to body, soul, and spirit. I take back everything that belongs to me body, soul, and spirit.

I renounce all judgements, demonic contracts, toxic vows, spoken and unspoken, that I've made regarding. I choose to divorce ______________ and all connected/affiliated satanic covens, groups, councils, networks and secret societies.

Holy Spirit, wash over and cleanse my mind and heart. Renew my thinking to align with truth. I repent for believing any lies because of this soul tie... I break the power of all lies... Holy Spirit what Truths do you want to reveal to me?

God, Jesus, Holy Spirit, I dedicate every part of myself to you. I ask that you anoint and cover my body, soul, and spirit with your oil that destroys the yoke of bondage. Glory of God Come. Holy Spirit baptize me. I thank you that in your presence is the fullness of freedom and joy!

I ask all of these things in Jesus' name. Jesus, what do you want to show me or say to me? Is there anything else I need to pray about regarding breaking this soul tie?

FORCED WILL PRAYER

God, I repent for all sins, transgressions, and iniquities that I have committed against You, others, or myself—whether in my body, spirit, or any part of my soul.

I repent for, renounce, and break agreement with all agreements, promises, covenants, contracts, access points, and permissions made when traffickers, abusers, Satanists, occult members, or witches forced my free will—whether through torture and pain, manipulation, programming, programming symbols or code words, trauma, threats, or relentless repetition. I was forced to answer the way they wanted me to, forced to agree with them, forced to make decisions that benefited them, forced to do things for them, forced to sign contracts, forced to sin, and forced to obey them as they carried out Satan's plans.

My free will has been violated in the following ways: (list every known area).

Jesus, I know that You will not violate or force my free will or decisions. I repent for every way that I have rejected Your truth, Your plans, Your help, Your conviction, Your instruction, Your presence, Your Word, and Your wisdom. I repent for any distance I have created on my end and for any prisons or walls I have built to keep You out of any part of my soul, body, or spirit. I repent for any ways that I have grieved the Holy Spirit.

Jesus, are there any demons that I need to renounce and command to leave my life as a result of my free will being violated? (Wait on the Lord's answer. If you don't get a response, move on. If you do, follow with: "I renounce and command '________' to get out in Jesus' name and do not return.")

I ask for justice to be carried out against every person and demon that has forced my will. I declare that from now on, I will make my own choices.

I ask for wisdom, understanding, discernment, and conviction to recognize when I am being tricked, seduced, manipulated, programmed, tempted, or deceived. I declare that previous trauma triggers, programming code words and symbols do not have power to control me anymore in Jesus' name.

I ask for healing and freedom in every area where the violation of my free will has brought damage, injury, pain, affliction, infirmity, or mental health challenges in my body, soul, and spirit.

I choose, of my own free will, not to split, fracture, or dissociate my soul when feeling triggered, overwhelmed, overstimulated, or stressed. I choose, of my own free will, for my spirit to remain in my body when experiencing these things. I choose, of my own free will, to love, bless, and forgive myself. I choose to remain aligned according to God's original design for my body, soul, and spirit.

In Jesus' name, I ask. Amen.

PRAYER FOR PEACEFUL SLEEP

On behalf of every part of my soul, spirit, and body, I repent for all sin, transgression, and iniquity. I declare that the true Jesus Christ is my Lord and Savior.

I release the Kingdom of Heaven on this property and the peace of Jesus Christ. I repent for all sin, transgression, and iniquity that has taken place on this property—all the way back to creation. This includes the property in the natural and in the spirit realm, above it all the way up to the third heaven, and below it. I bless this property and every item on it in the name of Jesus.

I apply the anointing oil of the Lord that destroys the yoke of bondage and the blood of Jesus over and surrounding this property. Jesus, I declare that You are a wall of fire around the perimeter of this property, and You are the glory in the midst.

I command everything from Satan's kingdom to leave this property—underneath it, above it, and in the spirit realm all the way up to the heavens, including the air—now, in the name of Jesus. I command all things from Satan's kingdom to go now to the place where the true Lord Jesus sends you.

I close all doors, portals, and access points to Satan's kingdom or anyone working for Satan, now, in the name of Jesus. I seal every door, gateway, portal, and access point with the blood of the Lamb and lock them by the authority in the name of Jesus.

I declare that this is an astral-projection-free zone. I establish that no human or demon is permitted to astral project here—during the day or while I sleep—in the authority and in the name of Jesus.

I place a signpost in the spirit realm outside this property declaring that if anyone attempts to enter through astral projection, their civil court contract with demons and principalities will be destroyed by the holy, all-consuming fire of God, and their silver cords will be cut. I also place a signpost in the spirit realm outside this property with the gospel of Jesus Christ.

I declare Proverbs 26:2—that a curse without cause will not land on me or anyone sleeping on this property, in the name of Jesus.

I choose to believe in faith, Lord, that Your authority and power are stronger than any power of Satan or his kingdom. I bind and rebuke all witchcraft, occult practices, and Satanism directed against me while I sleep, in the name of Jesus. I rebuke all demons sent to disrupt my sleep, in Jesus' name. I renounce all agreements with demons sent to interrupt my sleep, in Jesus' name.

I declare that when I lie down to sleep, I will have sweet rest, in Jesus' name. I declare that I sleep in the peace of God, surrounded by Your glory.

I speak healing over my physical body—over all hormones, chemicals, and anything within me that would interrupt my sleep. I command all pain and discomfort in my body to leave, in the name of Jesus. I receive the healing available to me through the finished work of the cross, in Jesus' name.

I declare that I have the mind of Christ. I choose to cast all my cares, worries, and anxieties on You, Jesus, because You care for me. I give You all the stress and everything on my to-do list. I trust You, Lord, with everything that concerns me.

I will sleep from the realm of the Kingdom of God—in righteousness, joy, peace, and power in the Holy Spirit, in Jesus' name.

I thank You for the armor of God that I am clothed in. I thank You for the robe of righteousness—Your righteousness, Jesus—that You have given me. I believe by faith that I am covered and clothed in armor and righteousness.

I thank You for the living water of the Holy Spirit within me, washing me and cleansing me. I declare that I sleep under the protection of Psalm 91, Psalm 121, and Psalm 27—surrounded by the living Word of God, in Jesus' name.

God, Jesus, and Holy Spirit, I declare that You are the only ones who have permission to give me dreams, lead me, and guide me as I sleep. I declare that nothing from Satan's kingdom or programming is permitted or allowed to lead, guide, or give me dreams, imagery, or trauma memories, in Jesus' name.

God, hide me in Your glory and Your presence as I rest.

In Jesus' name, amen.

COURTROOM OF HEAVEN PRAYER STRATEGY

"He said, 'The knowledge of the secrets of the kingdom of God has been given to you, but to others I speak in parables, so that, though seeing, they may not see; though hearing, they may not understand.'" -Luke 8:10

1. Jesus Prayer Strategy

Luke 18:1-8 "Then Jesus told his disciples a parable to show them that they should always pray and not give up. He said: "In a certain town, there was a judge who neither feared God nor cared what people thought. And there was a widow in that town who kept coming to him with the plea, 'Grant me justice against my adversary.' "For some time he refused. But finally, he said to himself, 'Even though I don't fear God or care what people think, yet because this widow keeps bothering me, I will see that she gets justice, so that she won't eventually come and attack me!'" And the Lord said, "Listen to what the unjust judge says. And will not God bring about justice for his chosen ones, who cry out to him day and night? Will he keep putting them off? I tell you, He will see that they get justice, and quickly. However, when the Son of Man comes, will he find faith on the earth?"

(Here, Jesus is teaching a strategy when praying for breakthrough... Courtroom Intercession)

Hebrews 4:16 "So let us come boldly to the throne of our gracious God. There we will receive his mercy, and we will find grace to help us when we need it most."

John 5:19 "So Jesus explained, "I tell you the truth, the Son can do nothing by himself. He does only what he sees the Father doing. Whatever the Father does, the Son also does."

John 12:49 "I don't speak on my own authority. The Father who sent me has commanded me what to say and how to say it."

Luke 21:15 "For I will give you a mouth and a wisdom which all of your adversaries will not be able to contradict or resist."

2. The Righteous Judge Father God = Righteous Judge

(Do a word search for "Righteous Judge" in scripture, over 70)

"But God is the Judge; He puts down one and exalts another." –Psalm 75:7

"I, even I, am He who blots out your transgressions for my own sake; And I will not remember your sins. Put Me in remembrance; Let us contend together; State your case, that you may be acquitted." –Isaiah 43:25-26 NKJV

"For the Lord is our Judge, The Lord is our King; He will save us." -Isaiah 33:22 "There is only one Lawgiver and Judge..." –James 4:12

"The Righteous Judge" – 2 Timothy 4:8

3. The Prosecuting Attorney Satan = Prosecuting Attorney, Accuser of the brethren, Adversary

Read all of Revelation 12:10-11 Accuser, accusing us day and night before God

Accuser= katēgoreō (Greek) = Before a judge: to make an accusation, of an extra-judicial accusation.

1 Peter 5:8 "Be sober, be vigilant; because your adversary the devil walks about like a roaring lion, seeking whom he may devour."

Adversary = Antidikos (Greek) =An Opponent in a lawsuit

"Like a fluttering sparrow or a darting swallow, an undeserved curse will not land on its intended victim." –Proverbs 26:2

(Once legal rights are broken through repentance and the Blood of Jesus)

Job 1:6-7 (The story of Job has some courtroom activity in it, where Satan comes before the Lord)

"Settle matters quickly with your adversary who is taking you to court. Do it while you are still together on the way, or your adversary may hand you over to the judge, and the judge may hand you over to the officer, and you may be thrown into prison." –Matthew 5:25 NIV

Matthew 18:21-35 (The importance of forgiving and releasing to be free)

4. Our Defense Attorney Lord Jesus = Defense Attorney, Advocate & Mediator

"Oh Lord, You have pleaded the case for my soul; You have redeemed my life. O Lord, You have seen how I am wronged; Judge my case." –Lamentations 3:58-59

"My dear children, I am writing this to you so that you will not sin. But if anyone does sin, we have an advocate who pleads our case before the Father. He is Jesus Christ, the one who is truly righteous."-1 John 2:1 NLT

"Therefore, he is able, once and forever, to save those who come to God through him. He lives forever to intercede with God on their behalf." –Hebrews 7:25

"You were dead because of your sins and because your sinful nature was not yet cut away. Then God made you alive with Christ, for he forgave all our sins. He canceled the record of the charges against us and took it away by nailing it to the cross. In this way, he disarmed the spiritual rulers and authorities. He shamed them publicly by his victory over them on the cross." –Colossians 2:13-15 5.

5. Defendant: Our role is as a "Minister of Reconciliation" vs. 20 " ' So we are Christ's ambassadors; God is making his appeal through us. We speak for Christ when we

plead, "Come back to God!" ' (READ ALL 2 Cor. 5:17-20 NLT & AMP)

"Shall the prey be taken from the mighty, or the lawful captive delivered? But thus saith the Lord, Even the captives of the mighty shall be taken away, and the prey of the terrible shall be delivered: for I will contend with him that contendeth with thee, and I will save thy children." -Isaiah 49:24-25

"When Job prayed for his friends, the Lord restored his fortunes. In fact, the Lord gave him twice as much as before!" –Job 42:10

"He will even deliver one who is not innocent; yes, he will be delivered by the purity of your hands."-Job 22:30

6. Law vs. New Covenant (Read the book of Romans and the Book of Galatians)

"a better covenant which contains far more wonderful promises" - Hebrews 8:6-9

"For sin will no longer be a master over you, since you are not under Law [as slaves], but under [unmerited] grace [as recipients of God's favor and mercy]. What then [are we to conclude]? Shall we sin because we are not under Law, but under [God's] grace? Certainly not! Do you not know that when you continually offer yourselves to someone to do his will, you are the slaves of the one whom you obey, either [slaves] of sin, which leads to death, or of obedience, which leads to righteousness (right standing with God)?" –Romans 6:14-16 AMP

"The sting of death is sin, and the strength of sin is the law. But thanks be to God, who gives us the victory through our Lord Jesus Christ." -1 Corinthians 15:56-57

"But those who depend on the law to make them right with God are under his curse, for the Scriptures say, "Cursed is everyone who does not observe and obey all the commands that are written in God's Book of the Law." So, it is clear that no one can be made right with God by trying to keep the law. For the Scriptures say, "It is through faith that a righteous person has life." This way of faith is very different from the way of law, which says, "It is through obeying the law that a person has life." –Galatians 3:10-12

7. A Beautiful Future Has Been Written for You

Psalm 139:16 "You saw me before I was born. Every day of my life was recorded in your book. Every moment was laid out before a single day had passed." (Do a study on the Books in heaven)

8. Courtroom Prayer Strategy:

I enter your gates with thanksgiving and your courts with praise. (Psalm 100:4)

I forgive and release those who have sinned against me. (Matt. 18:21-35)

I repent of all sin, transgressions and iniquity. (Acts 3:19) I repent of all word curses, judgements and accusations that I have spoken against myself or others... and that I have specifically spoken about the person(s) and situation(s) in my case today. (Prov. 6:2, James 5:9, Rom. 2:1, Prov. 18:20-21amp, Matt. 7:1-5, Luke 6:37-42, James 3:4-5)

I repent for every place that my words have not agreed with your Words, Jesus... I ask that the word of my testimony would be in agreement with the Word of your testimony, Jesus... (Rev. 12:10- 11)

I overcome the enemy by 1) the Blood of Jesus, 2) the word of my testimony, and 3) fully surrendering my life (loving not my life, even unto death).

I ask that you cleanse me with the Blood of Jesus that sets me free and washes away all of my sins. (1 John 1:7-9, Rev 1:5-6)

I ask that you lift any veils off my eyes and heart, that I may have clear revelation of truth and give me ears to hear what the Spirit of the Lord is saying. (2 Cor. 3:14-15 amp, Mark 4:9, Ephesians 1:17)

I ask that you give me wisdom. "For I will give you a mouth and a wisdom which all of your adversaries will not be able to contradict or resist." –Luke 21:15 I declare that I am the righteousness of Christ. (2 Cor. 5:21)

I declare that I am seated in heavenly places in Christ. (Ephes. 2:6)

I declare that I am not under the authority or the dominion of the kingdom of darkness, but I have been transferred into the Kingdom of Jesus. (Col. 1:13-14) I declare that I am a royalty in God's family. (Rev. 1:5-6, Rom. 8:15, 1 Pet. 2:9)

Father God, I ask that you cancel the accusers' case, and charges against me in Jesus' name according to Colossians 2:13-15 "You were dead because of your sins and because your sinful nature was not yet cut away. Then God made you alive with Christ, for he forgave all our sins. He canceled the record of the charges against us and took it away by nailing it to the cross. In this way, he disarmed the spiritual rulers and authorities. He shamed them publicly by his victory over them on the cross."

Pray in the Spirit (Romans 8:26-28)

Father God is there anything that you want to say to me or show me? Conclude by thanking and worship- ping God for all that He has done!

SAMPLE COURTROOM PRAYER JOURNAL NOTES

Date: ___________________

Primary Case (reason for entering): _______________

____

    *Pray a cleansing prayer like the one in #8 above
*Go boldly to the throne of our gracious God. There you will receive his mercy, and you will find grace to help you when you need it most. (Hebrews 4:16)

State your Case:_______________________________

____

____

____

Ask Father God to reveal the legal rights, accusations, and charges against the defendant. What access point is the enemy using? Repent, apply the Blood, declare the TRUTH. What did Father God reveal?

____

____

____

____

____

____

____

What did you hear, see, or encounter?

____

____

____

____

____

____

____

____

*Conclude with Praise, Thanksgiving and Worship
Was there a noticeable, tangible breakthrough after
this courtroom appointment?

____

____

____

____

____

____

____

____

____

INTRODUCTION TO GOD, JESUS AND HOLY SPIRIT

INTRODUCTION TO JESUS (YESHUA):

- Son of God (1 John 4:15)
- Savior (Acts 4:12)
- Light of the World (John 8:12)
- The Word of God (John 1:14)
- Truth (John 8:32)
- Redeemer (Job 19:25)
- Our Hope (1 Timothy 1:1)
- Friend (John 15:15)
- Advocate (1 John 2:1)
- Mediator (1 Timothy 2:5)
- Faithful and True (Rev. 19:11)
- Good Shepherd (John 10:11)
- Holy Servant (Acts 4:29-30)
- King of Kings (Revelation 17:14)
- The One who Sets You Free (John 8:36)
- Author and Perfecter of Our Faith (Hebrews 12:2)
- The One Who Gives Eternal Life (John 10:28-30)
- By His Wounds We are Healed (Isaiah 53:5)
- Our Victory (1 Corinthians 15:57)
- Meets our Needs (Philippians 4:9)
- Offering and Sacrifice to God (Ephesians 5:2)
- Prince of Peace (Isaiah 9:6)
- Immanuel "God with Us" (Isaiah 7:14)
- The Way, The Truth, The Life (John 14:6)

- The Door (John 10:9)
- Resurrection and the Life (John 11:25)
- The One with All Authority (Matthew 28:18)
- Lion of the Tribe of Judah (Revelation 5:5)
- Husband Bridegroom (Matthew 9:15)

INTRODUCTION TO HEAVENLY FATHER (GOD):

"To the fatherless, he is a father. To the widow, he is a champion friend. To the lonely, he makes them part of a family. To the prisoners, he leads into prosperity until they sing for joy. This is our Holy God in His Holy Place! But for the rebels, there is heartache and despair." (Psalm 68:5-6 TPT)

- God is Love (1 John 4:8)
- God is Holy (Isaiah 43:15)
- Ancient of Days (Daniel 7)
- Beginning and the End (Revelation 1:8)
- Creator (Genesis 1)
- Healer (Exodus 15:26)
- Defender (Deuteronomy 32:4)
- Light (1 John 1:5)
- Compassionate and Gracious, slow to anger, faithful (Exodus 34:5-7)
- The God who provides (Genesis 22:14)
- Defense, strength, salvation (Isaiah 12:2)
- The Rock (Isaiah 26:4)
- Most High (Psalm 83:18)

- Sovereign, greatness, strong hand (Deuteronomy 3:24)
- Consuming Fire, Jealous for us (Deuteronomy 4:24)
- Shield (Proverbs 30:5)
- Banner of Victory (Exodus 17:15)
- Peace (Judges 6:24)
- Wise (Romans 11:33-34)
- Counselor (Psalm 16:7)
- Everlasting Strength (Isaiah 26:4)
- God of Wonders (Psalm 40:5)

INTRODUCTION TO HOLY SPIRIT:

- The Holy Spirit Empowers You (Acts 1:8)
- Gives Life (John 6:63)
- Your Counselor and Helper (John 14:26)
- Comforter (John 14:16; John 14:26; John 15:26)
- Teacher (John 14:26)
- Resurrection Power (Romans 8:11)
- Testifies of Jesus (John 15:26)
- Gives Supernatural Gifts (1 Corinthians 12:8-10; Romans 12:6-7)
- Strengthens and Encourages (Acts 9:31)
- Leads and Guides (Romans 8:14)
- Reveals Truth (John 16:13)
- Helps You in Your Weaknesses (Romans 8:26)
- Intercedes (Romans 8:26)
- Searches the Deep Things of God (1 Corinthians 2:10)
- Sanctifies (1 Corinthians 6:11)
- Reminds You of the Word (John 14:26)

- Edifies You (1 Corinthians 14:4)
- Builds You Up (Jude 1:20)
- Gives You Rest (Isaiah 28)
- Refreshes You (Acts 3:19-21)
- Convicts and Forbids (John 16:8; Acts 16:6-7)
- Love, Joy, Peace, Patience, Kindness, Goodness, Faithfulness, Gentleness, Self Control (Galatians 5:22-23)
- Hovered Over the Waters of the Earth During Creation (Genesis 1:1-2)
- Took Part in the Conception of Jesus within a Virgin (Matthew 1:18)
- Present During the Baptism of Jesus (Matthew 3:16)
- Present During the Resurrection of Jesus (Romans 8:11)

Do not receive, tolerate, or be deceived by a different Jesus, a different spirit, or a false gospel. (1 Corinthians 11:3-4)

PRAYER:

Heavenly Father on behalf of every part of me, in every location, and on every timeline of my life...

- I repent for all sin, transgression, iniquity with every false God (Satan, demons and principalities), False Jesus, False Holy Spirit (Spirit Guides and Kundalini Spirit).
- I renounce and break agreement with them in Jesus' name. I stamp, with the blood of Jesus,

all agreements, contacts, and covenants made with them. I apply Colossians 2:14 15, nailing every accusation against me to the cross of the true Jesus Christ.

- I remove from every part of my soul, spirit and body all Satanic, demonic, and/or cursed gems, jewelry, devices, implants, clothing, seed, spiritual dust, food, drink and every other cursed item in me or on me from Satan's Kingdom. I remove it all and burn it with the fire of the Holy Spirit, never to return to me in Jesus name. (Remove all of these items from your home, vehicle and possessions. Keeping them is a sign of covenant and agreement. Get rid of them immediately.)
- I divorce, evict and command all false god's, false Jesus', false Holy Spirits to leave every part of my life now and go to where the true Lord Jesus sends you.
- I renounce all lies and programming that I learned from them, all images and memories they have shown me in Jesus' name. I deinstall and remove all of the effects of these lies and programming in Jesus' name.
- I renounce all false spiritual gifts and I ask for a washing and cleansing of my true spiritual gifts, given to me by the Holy Spirit.
- Baptize me in the Holy Spirit and give me a heavenly language/tongues.
- I receive you Heavenly Father, Jesus and Holy Spirit to be the leadership of my life.

HEALING MIRACLE DECLARATIONS

"But he was pierced for our rebellion, crushed for our sins. He was beaten so we could be whole. He was whipped so we could be healed." (Isaiah 53:5)

"He personally carried our sins in his body on the cross so that we can be dead to sin and live for what is right. By his wounds you are healed." (1 Peter 2:24)

- By Your stripes, Jesus, I am healed. Thank You for paying the price for my healing. (Isaiah 53:5)
- The healing of the Lord will spring forth speedily. (Isaiah 58:8)
- I cried out to You, God, and You healed me. (Psalms 30:2-3)
- God, I call on You in my day of trouble and I know You will deliver me. I glorify You. (Psalm 50:15)
- My healing has already been provided in the atonement. (Matthew 8:17)
- You will take sickness away from me (Exodus 23:20-25; Deuteronomy 7:12-15)
- Father God, Your Word is life to me and health to all my flesh. (Proverbs 4:22)
- According to my own faith, I am healed. (Matthew 9:22, 29)
- I praise You, Lord, and forget not all of Your benefits, that You forgive all of my sins and heal all of my diseases. Thank You for redeeming my

life from the pit and crowning me with love and compassion. (Psalm 103:2-4)

- I have been given a spirit of power, love, and a sound mind. (2 Timothy 1:7)
- I am spiritually clean. My old self has been removed. (Colossians 2:11)
- I am born again in Christ, and the evil one, the devil, cannot touch me. (1 John 5:18)
- No weapon formed against me shall prosper. (Isaiah 54:17)
- I can do all things through Christ who strengthens me. (Philippians 4:13)
- I have the Victory. (1 Corinthians 15:57)
- I am more than a Conqueror. (Romans 8:37)
- The weapons of my warfare are mighty through God. (2 Corinthians 10:4)
- Greater is He that's in me than he who is in the world. (1 John 4:4)
- The Lord is the strength of my life; Of whom shall I be afraid? (Psalm 27:1)
- When I speak the Word, it is quick, and powerful and sharper than a two-edged sword. (Hebrews 4:12)
- I am a Disciple of Jesus, so I have authority over every unclean spirit and all sickness and diseases. (Matthew 10:1; Mark 3:14-15; Mark 6:7; Luke 9:1)
- Father God, forgive me of all my sins. I choose to forgive and release everyone who has ever sinned against me. (Matthew 18:21-35, Matthew 6:9-13, Luke 5:17-26)

Additional Instruction for Healing in the Word of God:

- Call for the elders of the church to pray for you, anoint you with oil, and lay hands on you for healing. (James 5:14; Mark 16:18)
- Confess your faults one to another and pray for each other that ye may be healed. (James 5:16)
- Understand the healing that comes through taking Communion. (1 Corinthians 11:27-30)
- Repent from all sin in your life and go and sin no more. Sin is sometimes related to sickness. (Mark 2:5)
- Forgive those who have sinned against you. Sometimes unforgiveness keeps us imprisoned. (Matthew 18:21-35)

SPIRITUAL WARFARE DECLARATIONS

- I am a new person. My past is forgiven and everything is new. (2 Corinthians 5:17)
- I am a child of light and not darkness. (1 Thessalonians 5:5)
- The sinful person I used to be died with Christ, and sin no longer rules my life. (Romans 6:1-6)
- I am free from the punishment (condemnation) my sin deserves. (Romans 8:1)
- I have been given the mind of Christ. He gives me His wisdom to make right choices. (1 Corinthians 2:16)
- I may approach God with boldness, freedom, and confidence. (Ephesians 3:12)
- I have been rescued from the dark power of Satan's rule and have been brought into the kingdom of Christ. (Colossians 1:13)

- I have been forgiven of all of my sins and set free. The debt against me has been cancelled. (Colossians 1:14)
- I have been given a spirit of power, love, and a sound mind. (2 Timothy 1:7)
- I am born again in Christ, and the evil one, the devil, cannot touch me. (1 John 5:18)
- No weapon formed against me shall prosper. (Isaiah 54:17)
- I can do all things through Christ who strengthens me. (Philippians 4:13)
- I have the victory! (1 Corinthians 15:57)
- I am more than a conqueror. (Romans 8:37)
- The weapons of my warfare are mighty through God. (2 Corinthians 10:4)
- I am seated with Christ in heavenly realms. (Ephesians 2:6)
- Greater is He that's in me than he who is in the world. (1 John 4:4)
- The Lord is the strength of my life; Of whom shall I be afraid? (Psalm 27:1)
- When I speak the Word, it is quick, and powerful, and sharper than a two-edged sword. (Hebrews 4:12)
- I am a disciple of Jesus, so I have authority over every unclean spirit and all sickness and diseases. (Matthew 10:1; Mark 3:14 15; Mark 6:7; Luke 9:1)

KINGDOM OF GOD SCRIPTURE DECLARATIONS

1. "I seek first the Kingdom of God and His righteousness, and all my needs are provided." (Matthew 6:33 TPT)
2. "When I actively demonstrate the Kingdom of God, my words are full of explosive power." (1 Corinthians 4:20 TPT).
3. "The Kingdom of God is within me, and I carry it wherever I go." (Luke 17:21 TPT)
4. "I cherish the Kingdom of Heaven like a hidden treasure and am willing to give up everything for it." (Matthew 13:44 TPT)
5. "The Kingdom of Heaven starts small like a mustard seed, but grows into a large tree that provides refuge for many." (Matthew 13:31-32 TPT)
6. "I am humble like a child, and I am great in the Kingdom of Heaven." (Matthew 18:3 TPT)
7. "I am not afraid, for it is my Father's good pleasure to give me the Kingdom." (Luke 12:32 TPT)
8. "I am born again, and I can see the Kingdom of God." (John 3:3 TPT)
9. "I am blessed by my Father, and I am invited to inherit the Kingdom prepared for me since the foundation of the world." (Matthew 25:34 TPT)
10. "I am poor in spirit, I know that everything of value I have is found in Christ, and the Kingdom of Heaven is mine." (Matthew 5:3 TPT)
11. "The Kingdom of Heaven is like a merchant seeking beautiful pearls, and when he finds

one of great value, he sells everything he has to buy it." (Matthew 13:45-46 TPT)

12. "I am a sower of good seed, contributing to the growth of the Kingdom of Heaven." (Matthew 13:37-38 TPT)

13. "The Kingdom of Heaven suffers violence, and the violent take it by force." (Matthew 11:12 TPT)

14. "I am a laborer in the harvest, sent out by the Lord of the harvest to gather souls for the Kingdom of Heaven." (Matthew 9:37-38 TPT)

15. "I will forgive others from my heart, just as my heavenly Father forgives me, and I will be forgiven in the Kingdom of Heaven." (Matthew 18:21-35 TPT)

16. "As I love and serve others, I am serving Christ and will be rewarded in the Kingdom of Heaven." (Matthew 25:31-46 TPT)

17. "I will be a peacemaker, for they shall be called the children of God and inherit the Kingdom of Heaven." (Matthew 5:9 TPT)

RIGHTEOUSNESS SCRIPTURE DECLARATIONS

1. "I am completely forgiven and set free from my past sins." (Ephesians 1:7, TPT)

2. "I am made righteous and clean through faith in Jesus Christ." (Romans 3:22, TPT)

3. "I am a new creation in Christ, the old has gone, and the new has come." (2 Corinthians 5:17, TPT)

4. "I am not condemned but justified by faith in Jesus." (Romans 8:1, TPT)

5. "My sins are washed away by the blood of Jesus, and I am cleansed." (1 John 1:7, TPT)
6. "I have been brought into the family of God and am now His child." (John 1:12, TPT)
7. "I have been redeemed from the curse of the law and its shame." (Galatians 3:13, TPT)
8. "I am no longer a slave to sin but have been set free to live a righteous life." (Romans 6:18, TPT)
9. "I have been crucified with Christ, and it is no longer I who live, but Christ lives in me." (Galatians 2:20, TPT)
10. "I am now seated with Christ in the heavenly realms, far above all shame and disgrace." (Ephesians 2:6, TPT)
11. "I am accepted and loved by God just as I am." (Romans 15:7, TPT)
12. "I am clothed with the robe of righteousness given to me by Jesus." (Isaiah 61:10, TPT)
13. "I am an overcomer through the power of Jesus Christ, who has defeated shame and sin on my behalf." (1 John 5:4, TPT)
14. "I have been given the righteousness of Christ, so I can boldly approach the throne of grace." (Hebrews 4:16, TPT)
15. "I am no longer defined by my past but by the finished work of the cross." (Philippians 3:13-14, TPT)
16. "He has forgiven me for all my sins and removed them as far as the east is from the west." (Psalm 103:12, TPT)
17. "I have been chosen by God, and He will not abandon me." (Isaiah 41:9, TPT)

18. "I am skillfully and wonderfully made by God, and He delights in me." (Psalm 139:14, TPT)
19. "The Lord has plans for my life, filled with hope and a future." (Jeremiah 29:11, TPT)
20. "I am convinced that God will completely finish the excellent work He began in me." (Philippians 1:6, TPT)
21. "The Lord is my strength and my shield, and I can trust in Him with all my heart." (Psalm 28:7, TPT)
22. "I am the Lord's servant, and He will guide me in His perfect plan for my life." (Psalm 32:8, TPT)
23. "I am surrounded by the Lord's passionate love, and He will never let me go." (Psalm 32:10, TPT)
24. "The Lord is my light and my salvation, and I have nothing to fear." (Psalm 27:1, TPT)
25. "I am God's poetry, created in Christ Jesus for good works that He has prepared for me to do." (Ephesians 2:10, TPT)
26. "The Lord will fight for me, and I can be still and know that He is in control." (Exodus 14:14, TPT)
27. "God is my refuge and strength, and I can find safety in Him." (Psalm 46:1, TPT)
28. "I have been set free from the snare of the enemy, and my soul finds rest in God alone." (Psalm 25:15; 62:1, TPT)
29. "I am convinced that nothing can ever separate me from the endless love of God revealed in Christ Jesus our Lord." (Romans 8:38-39, TPT)
30. "I am blessed when I hunger and thirst for righteousness. I will be filled." (Matthew 5:6)

REGULATING THE NERVOUS SYSTEM TOOLS

1. Grounding with the 5-4-3-2-1 Technique

When you feel anxious, disconnected, or overwhelmed:
- 5 things you can see – Look around and name five visible things.
- 4 things you can touch – Touch items near you (chair, table, your clothing).
- 3 things you can hear – Tune in to external sounds.
- 2 things you can smell – Notice scents around you, or recall a comforting smell.
- 1 thing you can taste – Take a sip of water or recall the taste of something pleasant.

A simpler version of this exercise is to focus on three things around you and intentionally engage your senses, focusing on how those items look, feel, smell, etc.

This helps bring the body back to the present moment and signals safety.

2. Name of God Breathwork (Yahweh, Jesus, Yeshua)

Proverbs 18:10 NASB

"The name of the Lord is a strong tower; The righteous runs into it and is safe."

- Breathe in slowly for 3 seconds
- Hold for 3 seconds
- Breathe out slowly for 3 seconds
- Speak the name of God, and repeat for several rounds.

3. Scripture Visualization Encounter

"Pour out all your worries and stress upon Him and leave them there, for He always tenderly cares for you." – 1 Peter 5:7 (TPT)

- What does it look like for you to pour out your worries and stress to Jesus right now?
- Ask Jesus to help you picture yourself handing Him specific burdens or concerns.
- Ask Jesus, "What do you want to reveal (show or say) to me?
- Ask Jesus, "What do you want to give me to fill the space of what I just released to you?"

4. Move Your Body And Shift Your Sensory Input

When your nervous system is dysregulated... whether you're anxious, frozen, overwhelmed, or numb... gently moving your body or changing your environment can help restore a sense of safety and calm. Movement communicates to your body that it is no longer in danger.

Simple ways to reset your nervous system:

- Take a slow walk outdoors and notice what you see, hear, and smell.
- Step into the shower and feel the water run over your skin—it can provide a full sensory reset.
- Stretch, sway side to side, or shake out your hands to release built-up tension.
- Turn on peaceful worship music or nature sounds to help calm auditory input.
- Open a window or step outside to breathe in fresh air.

5. Tool: Create a Sensory Reset Kit

"Be still and know that I am God." – Psalm 46:10 (TPT)

A Sensory Reset Kit is a small collection of items that help ground you when your nervous system feels overwhelmed or shut down. It's a practical way to shift your sensory input and invite regulation through calm, familiar, and pleasant sensations.

What to Include in Your Kit (Customize Based on Your Needs):

Touch (Tactile Grounding)
* Fidget toy or stress ball
* Soft piece of fabric (like velvet or satin)

Smell (Aromatherapy And Memory Triggers)
* Essential oils (lavender, peppermint, eucalyptus, frankincense)
* Scented lotion
* Herbal tea bags (chamomile, mint, citrus)

Taste (Instant Grounding And Focus)
* Strong mints or sour candies
* Herbal teas or flavored water packets
* Ginger chews or gum

Hearing (Auditory Regulation)
* Small earbuds and a worship or instrumental playlist
* Sound machine or calming nature sound app
* Personalized voice recording with a prayer or scripture

Sight (Visual Calm And Focus)
* Scripture or encouraging quote cards
* Photos of peaceful places or loved ones
* Calming images or nature cards
* Art supplies to color

STATEMENTS OF LEGALISM AND A RELIGIOUS SPIRIT OR MINDSET AND FREEDOM PRAYER

1. "If others haven't followed the same path I did to become righteous, they aren't truly free." Implies that salvation or freedom is achievable only through rigid conformity rather than grace.

2. "I can tell who is close to God by their actions, and some people clearly are not as close to God as they say."
   Judges people's spiritual closeness to God by their outward actions instead of the heart.
3. "People who are joyful and carefree in their faith just don't take God seriously enough."
   Looks down on childlike faith and joy, often resenting spontaneity and grace.
4. "If I'm not in control, I worry that things won't be done the right way—God's way."
   Links control to perceived righteousness, struggling to trust in God's leading.
5. "Those I minister to should stay under my guidance, or else they'll likely fall away."
   Believes that success in faith is tied to their authority, downplaying the Holy Spirit's work in others.
6. "It's important for people to see the sacrifices I've made to live righteously."
   Focuses on outward demonstrations of faith as a measure of godliness, seeking recognition.
7. "If someone isn't following religious rules, they aren't showing respect for God."
   Places emphasis on legalistic practices rather than the heart or spirit of the law.
8. "I struggle to be patient with people who just don't get the importance of obedience like I do."

Exhibits a lack of grace and understanding toward those at different stages in their faith.

9. "I need to make sure others understand that my way of following God is the most faithful way."
   Assumes that personal convictions are universal standards everyone should follow.

10. "People who break from tradition are jeopardizing the integrity of our faith."
    Views traditional practices as essential to faith, disregarding flexibility in personal convictions.

11. "I have a duty to point out sin in others so they don't stray from God."
    Feels a responsibility to police others' actions, often to the point of legalistic correction.

12. "It's not really godly to associate with people who don't live up to our moral standards."
    Excludes those who seem unworthy by personal standards, rather than showing compassion or love.

13. "If that person were truly close to God, they wouldn't spend time with people like that."
    This implies that someone's spiritual standing is tarnished by their associations, overlooking Jesus' example of reaching out with compassion and love to those on the margins.

14. "God only works in the ways I've experienced Him before. If someone claims to encounter God differently, it's probably not genuine."
    This perspective limits God to past experiences and dismisses the possibility of Him working in fresh or unexpected ways, disregarding His boundless nature.

15. "No matter how much I do, I'll never measure up—and I often feel others fall short, too."
    This mindset stems from perfectionism and self-criticism, often projecting the same harsh judgment onto others, rather than embracing grace and the freedom it brings.

16. "I can't risk anyone knowing about my private struggles—maintaining my public image is too important."
    This attitude prioritizes appearances over authenticity, driven by fear of vulnerability and a desire to appear flawless, often at the expense of genuine connection and growth.

17. "It's important that I get credit for the things I do. Bringing attention to myself is a way of receiving the honor I deserve."
    This mindset seeks validation through recognition, often prioritizing personal acknowledgment over humility or service for its own sake.

PRAYER:

Father God, I pray on behalf of every part of me, in every location and on every timeline of my life...

-I repent for all sin with or for the spirit of legalism and the religious spirit.

-I repent for all agreements and covenants with the spirit of legalism and the religious spirit.

-I renounce every legalistic lie and thought process.

-I choose to forgive all people who introduced me to legalism and religion.

-I repent for and renounce pride and making myself an Idol.

-I repent for every way that I have taken credit or glory that belongs to you, Lord.

-Give me a fresh baptism of the Holy Spirit, Jesus.

-Give me childlike faith to enter into the fullness of the Kingdom of God.

-I choose to accept your righteousness, Jesus. Thank you for giving me a robe of righteousness.

In Jesus' name!

ABOUT THE AUTHOR

Sula Lael's passion for helping others comes from overcoming a very painful past. She has found freedom and healing from the traumas of her life and has been radically transformed through becoming a fiery believer and a follower of Jesus Christ. Her life exudes joy and peace, which is present in all that she does as a Transformation Strategist, Trafficking Survivor Expert, and Freedom Empowerment Consultant!

She works to spread awareness, teach prevention, and equip nonprofits and service providers in the anti-trafficking movement through training and consulting. With a wealth of experience, she has aided countless survivors of exploitation and occult ritual abuse in escape, healing, and transition to a renewed life.

It is her joy to advance the Kingdom of God with the love and power of the Gospel. She ministers in faith to see Jesus miraculously heal many. She is an accomplished author of six books with more on the way! Additionally, she started a 501c3 Nonprofit called Take Flight Survivors in 2022.

You can read her full story in her book titled, "Fighting for Your Purpose – From Sex Trafficking to Ministry."

www.SulaLael.com
www.TakeFlightSurvivors.org

Instagram @SulaLael & @TakeFlightSurvivors